ROLE-PLAYING METHODS IN THE CLASSROOM

TEACHER RESOURCE BOOKLETS ON CLASSROOM
SOCIAL RELATIONS AND LEARNING

Role-Playing Methods in the Classroom

MARK CHESLER and ROBERT FOX

Center for Research on Utilization of Scientific Knowledge
Institute for Social Research
University of Michigan

74059

Science Research Associates, Inc. Chicago

A Subsidiary of IBM

Part of the research reported herein was supported through the Cooperative Research Program of the Office of Education, U.S. Department of Health, Education, and Welfare, under Contract SAE 9159. Under the terms of that contract the federal government has a royalty-free license to the use of the material contained herein which appeared in any reports to the federal government under the above-mentioned contract.

The publisher gratefully acknowledges the copyright holders' permissions to quote and summarize:
—From *Human Nature and the Social Order,* by C. H. Cooley. (Copyright 1902, 1922, Charles Scribner's Sons.) Adapted and summarized with the permission of Charles Scribner's Sons.
—From *Mind, Self and Society,* by G. H. Mead. Copyright 1934, University of Chicago Press.
—From "Preliminary Investigation of the Relation of Insight and Empathy," by R. A. Dymond, *Journal of Consulting Psychology,* Vol. 12, 1948.
—From *Principles of Human Relations: Applications to Management,* by N. R. F. Maier. Copyright 1952, John Wiley & Sons, Inc. Reprinted by permission.
—From *Psychodrama,* Volume I, by J. L. Moreno, M.D., 1946, Beacon House Inc., publishers.
—From *Social Learning and Imitation,* by N. Miller and J. Dollard. Copyright 1941, Yale University Press. Reprinted by permission.
—From *Some Notes on How to Use Role Playing,* by P. Rosenberg. Copyright 1950, National Training Laboratories.

PREFACE

The teacher who wants to keep abreast of new knowledge in the behavioral sciences and utilize it to improve his teaching techniques and professional effectiveness faces a formidable challenge. Fortunately this challenge is not solely the teacher's responsibility. Scientists from the various disciplines are seeking ways of collaborating with educational specialists to apply developments in the behavioral sciences to the classroom and to improve channels of communication to teachers.

Role-Playing Methods in the Classroom is one of three TEACHER RESOURCE BOOKLETS ON CLASSROOM SOCIAL RELATIONS AND LEARNING that grew out of such a cooperative research effort. At the Center for Research on Utilization of Scientific Knowledge at the University of Michigan, a team of social scientists and educational specialists for over a decade has been exploring some of the possibilities for cooperative research in the behavioral sciences and the application of the results of such research to the classroom. The projects have been supported by the U.S. Office of Education,* the National Institute of Mental Health,† and the McGregor Foundation.

The relation between classroom interpersonal relations and the effective learning of subject matter has been investigated through research questions such as these: What effect does the social power or social acceptance possessed or lacked by students have on their learning? What are the dynamics that make it difficult for a socially ineffective child to improve his status in the group? What kind of perceptions and expectations do teachers and students have of one another? What are the effects of children of different ages learning together? How can the socially ineffective child be helped to use his learning potential better?

Data have been gathered from several hundred classrooms through the use of diagnostic tools dealing with classroom social structures; individual and group attitudes toward learning; significant environmental forces influencing both teachers and students; and the nature of the student-teacher interaction. On the basis of these data the teachers participating in the research projects modified many of the preliminary diagnostic instruments and developed plans for altering their teaching methods to improve the learning climate of the classroom. Much ingenuity was shown by the participating teachers in taking the step from "What do the data say?" to "What can be done in my classroom to improve mental

*OE contract SAE 9159.
†NIMH grants M 919, OM 376, and MH 01780-08.

health and learning?" Further data were then gathered, again through the use of diagnostic tools, on the success or failure of the various plans and teaching methods that were developed.

This series of TEACHER RESOURCE BOOKLETS ON CLASSROOM SOCIAL RELATIONS AND LEARNING will present some of the knowledge gained from those studies.

Problem Solving to Improve Classroom Learning is the most comprehensive of the three booklets. It describes the whole problem-solving sequence, from perception of classroom difficulties through the evaluation of the remedial action taken. It deals with the issues of identifying problems in classroom life; selecting or developing appropriate diagnostic tools to analyze these problems; using diagnostic data and behavioral science resources to develop a plan for improving the learning atmosphere in the classroom; carrying out planned changes in classroom life; and evaluating the changes. Practical illustrations were provided by a variety of teachers and students who participated in the research projects.

Diagnosing Classroom Learning Environments focuses upon one stage of the problem-solving sequence—the process of getting reliable information about the actual state of affairs in the classroom. It presents and discusses some of the data-gathering instruments and techniques that have proved useful; it also provides suggestions on organizing the data so that the teacher can focus his efforts on changing the classroom learning environment.

Role-Playing Methods in the Classroom is about a technique that has proved highly useful to many teachers for dealing with a variety of classroom problems and reaching certain learning objectives. The booklet discusses the theoretical background of role playing and gives a step-by-step discussion of how to use role playing in the classroom. There are sample role-playing situations; suggestions on how to get started; advice on when to be cautious; discussions of the appropriateness of role playing for children of various ages and backgrounds; and case studies of groups of teachers and students using role playing under a variety of circumstances and for a variety of reasons.

The three booklets were written to complement each other. Since *Problem Solving* describes the whole problem-solving sequence in the classroom, it would be advantageous to read it first. It will provide an overview of the series and give the general framework of processes and concepts into which the other two booklets fit. However, although it describes a variety of methods designed to improve the classroom learning atmosphere, it does not do so with the extensive discussion and wealth of illustrative material that is focused upon one such method in *Role-Playing Methods*. And although *Role-Playing Methods* describes in detail one method of working with classroom problems, it has no extended treatment of how these problems are discovered, of how data are gathered about the problems, or of how progress is to be measured. For a detailed analysis of problem-discovery and data-gathering techniques, the reader is referred to *Diagnosing Classroom Learning Environments*.

The reader who wants to examine the theories and the research findings on which these three booklets are based is advised to turn to *Understanding Classroom Social Relations and Learning*.* The theories that relate classroom interpersonal relations and subject-matter learning are fully elaborated in that book, and the results of ten years of research in the schools to investigate the validity of these theories are presented.

The degree to which the school should be allowed to inquire into the personal and interpersonal life of the student is occasionally questioned. Articles have been written about the dangers of psychological tests, and legislation has been introduced in some states to restrict or prevent teachers and scientists from obtaining and utilizing such information. This matter is of fundamental concern for teachers who would act upon the suggestions in this series of booklets.

The research findings described in *Understanding Classroom Social Relations and Learning* give major support to the desirability of vigorous efforts on the part of the school and the teacher to understand and improve the mental health and learning climate of the classroom. The research has found that the mentally healthy student does learn academic subject matter better. Teachers who can diagnose and improve the learning atmosphere of their classrooms can thereby be better teachers. Accordingly, the teaching profession would be wise to extend its understanding of classroom social procedures and the techniques for dealing with them, while at the same time exercising caution so that the use of these techniques is not extended beyond the teacher's competence and the limits of the educational environment.

Unprofessional use of information about students and unwise applications of diagnostic data by teachers can be greatly reduced by better teacher training, by providing more focused and usable diagnostic materials, and by opening the channels of communication between the social scientist and the teacher. The materials in this series of booklets and the research on which they are based are directed toward these goals.

We wish to acknowledge the extensive teamwork that has made these research projects possible. In addition to the coauthors of this booklet, Mark Chesler and Robert Fox, other senior collaborators in the projects

---

*Lippitt, Fox, Schmuck, and Van Egmond (Chicago: Science Research Associates, 1966).

have been Mabel Kaufman, Ronald Lippitt, Margaret Barron Luszki, Richard Schmuck, and Elmer Van Egmond. The secretarial work has been led with dedication by Karen Donahue. If it were possible, each classroom teacher, each principal, each interviewer, each statistician, and each social scientist who made his unique contribution would be introduced to the reader by name. That so many should become so highly involved in an effort requiring extensive time beyond the usual demands, and professional skill beyond that normally expected, speaks well of their concern for the ideas presented in this series of booklets. We hope their efforts are rewarded by your finding *Role-Playing Methods in the Classroom* truly helpful.

RONALD LIPPITT
ROBERT FOX
Program Coordinators

TABLE OF CONTENTS

Preface v

CHAPTER ONE

Introduction

The dialogue that follows took place in a fourth-grade classroom. The teacher, Mrs. Adams, attempted to solve a problem in interpersonal relations by using a dramatic technique of classroom instruction.

MRS. ADAMS: We've been talking about problems that boys and girls have in getting along with others who are a few years older or younger than they are. Today let's see whether we can show what might happen to cause problems between fourth-grade students and sixth-graders. (*She places a chair in front of the room.*)

Let's pretend that this (*pointing to the chair*) is a hill. It's been snowing for a couple of days, and many boys and girls like to come here with their sleds. Now suppose there are two fourth-graders sledding. They have only one sled, so they've been riding double. They have just run into a rock, which has bent the runner so that the sled doesn't work. They try to fix it—to bend it back into shape— but they can't. Then they see two sixth-graders coming over the hill. Each sixth-grader has a new sled that he is eager to try out.

One of the fourth-graders thinks she should ask the sixth-graders for help; the other one isn't sure the older children will help. He doesn't see any point in asking, but the first one decides to ask for help anyway.

Let's see what would happen. Who would like to be a fourth-grader? . . . All right, Danny and Linda will be the fourth-graders. How about sixth-graders? . . . All right, Leon and Gwen, you are the sixth-graders. Fine. The class members who do not have parts will be the audience. You should watch the actors carefully. See if they play

1

their parts as you think boys and girls you know would actually behave. Think about what other things they could do to solve their problem.

Let's start the skit, Danny and Linda, with your being two typical fourth-graders named Fred and Florence. You are talking with each other before the sixth-graders appear. Come on up to the front of the room on this "hill." Leon and Gwen, you are two sixth-graders named Stan and Susan, and you come over to the hill later.

FLORENCE (*fourth grade*): I'm sorry your sled broke; we shouldn't have been riding double.

FRED (*fourth grade*): That's O.K., it wasn't your fault. It's an old sled anyway.

FLORENCE (*fourth grade*): Maybe we can fix it. . . . No, I can't do it. There are some sixth-graders; maybe they can help us fix it.

FRED (*fourth grade*): Ah, no. Let's not ask those big kids. They won't help; they won't do anything.

FLORENCE (*fourth grade*): Well, I'm going to ask them. Maybe they will help us. (*To Stan and Susan.*) Will you help us fix our sled?

STAN (*sixth grade*): Ah, that old sled? It looks like it belongs in a junkyard. It's not worth being fixed.

FRED (*fourth grade*): Yeah? We went all the way to that tree on it. That's farther than you can go on your sled.

STAN (*sixth grade*): Look what they think is far! All the way down to that tree! That's as far as their old sled can go. Ha!

FLORENCE (*fourth grade*): I'd like to see you go that far, you big fat . . .

SUSAN (*sixth grade*): C'mon, Stan, let's go.

FRED (*fourth grade*): (*Motion of grabbing Stan's sled.*) There, now I've pushed your sled down the hill.

STAN (*sixth grade*): Listen you, go get my sled.

FRED (*fourth grade*): I won't.

STAN (*sixth grade*): You'd better!

SUSAN (*sixth grade*): C'mon, let's slide down on my sled together. We can get yours all right. What did you want to mess around with these little kids for?

STAN (*sixth grade*): Yeah, O.K. They're not worth bothering with.

FRED (*fourth grade*): (*After Stan and Susan have gone.*) I knew we shouldn't have asked them to help.

FLORENCE (*fourth grade*): I didn't think they'd start teasing us.

FRED (*fourth grade*): Those kids, they think they're so big. Big kids are always looking for a fight.

FLORENCE (*fourth grade*): You shouldn't have pushed his sled down the hill, though.

FRED (*fourth grade*): Well, they deserved it. We can't get our sled fixed now.

MRS. ADAMS: Let's stop the skit here and give the rest of the class a chance to tell us how they feel. You four did a fine job; thank you.

This teacher attempted to deal with a recurrent problem of inter-personal rivalry and aggression between her own fourth-grade students and older students in the school by using role playing. She constructed a dramatic situation that set the stage for conflict, and she asked her students to play the parts of the characters. The classroom discussion that followed this improvisation involved the entire class in considering the behavior they had just witnessed. Both audience and actors suggested several alternative courses of action.

Many teachers have used role playing effectively to help solve class-room interpersonal problems and to teach human-relations skills in the classroom. Role playing also has been used to facilitate subject-matter learning through the dramatization of literary and historical works and historical or current events. In all these uses, role playing provides the student with a dramatic confrontation and clarification of (1) his relations with others, (2) his information about and expectations of society, (3) his evaluation of himself and his life style, and (4) the ways in which academic material may be relevant to his daily tasks.

Basically, role playing calls for a student's stepping outside the accustomed role that he plays in life, relinquishing his usual patterns of behavior in exchange for the role and patterns of another person. This other role may be that of a real person or may be entirely fictitious. In the opening dialogue the characters and the situation were fictitious, but the action it was designed to illustrate was a modification of actual student behavior the teacher had observed in the schoolyard. The student assumes the role of another person in the present or at a different time and place. He attempts, as far as possible, to speak like the other person, to behave like the other person, and to feel like the other person: this is the key to successful role playing. Since the student's own behavior is not at issue, he need not defend against appearing foolish or being censured. Thus the actor-students, the teacher, and the audience can observe and comment more objectively on the behaviors produced.

The role-playing technique has been used successfully in a variety of situations and institutions. It has been used in the settlement of tedious labor-management disputes to provide a way for each side to understand the position, feelings, and behaviors of the other side. This has not meant that the conflicts disappeared or the positions automatically changed; it has meant that both parties better understood each other's concerns and interests and were able to deal with each other with greater honesty and patience. Role playing has also been used at universities to stimulate learning and to create better understanding among members of student, faculty, and administrative bodies. Social scientists have used forms of role playing in colleges and institutes to present national and international problems and to experiment with new policies and strategies in group relations. Social scientists, welfare workers, and psychological counselors have used the technique in an attempt to help their students or clients gain greater insight into the nature of society and the dynamics of their own and other persons' behaviors.

This booklet describes the uses of role playing in the elementary and secondary school classroom. Chapter Two presents some social-psychological theory underlying the development and practice of role playing. Although an understanding of this material is not necessary for learning the methodology of role playing, it is valuable as a theoretical orientation to the technique. The following chapters concentrate on—

- The adaptability of role playing to elementary and secondary school classrooms, including its boundaries; its scope as a teaching aid; the means of assessing its potential use in the particular classroom; the ways a teacher may gain security in using it; and the general procedures for conducting role-playing sessions.
- Some case studies of the classroom use of role playing, selected to cover several areas of student life.
- A full description of the step-by-step procedures illustrated in the case studies, including suggestions for setting up and conducting each step; variations in each step that particular classroom situations may necessitate; and methods for evaluating the effects of the role-playing experience on student-student and student-teacher relations or on even broader student learning.

As a resource for the teacher who may wish to experiment with role playing, the Appendix contains many different situations and problem stories that can be used in the classroom. The Annotated Bibliography summarizes the contents of several books and articles relevant to the theory and practice of role playing, describing experiments in many areas of life. Finally, the Index is organized to guide the person new to role playing to the answers to many of the questions he may have. Throughout the booklet the authors have attempted to use material relevant to the classroom situation as the teacher and pupils experience it, and to be faithful to the body of appropriate research and theory developed by social scientists and educators.

4

CHAPTER TWO

Theoretical Foundations of Role Playing

The various uses of role playing have evolved from substantial theory and research on social relations and social interaction, the universal experience of all people, beginning with the young child's awakening to the social world around him and continuing throughout his life.

Human maturation is more than a process of learning "things"; it involves the gradual creation of a "role," a unique and accustomed manner of relating to "others"—persons, things, situations—outside the self that will determine and characterize all of a person's social behavior. Part of growing up is the learning and developing of this role, not solely as a factor of social status or social identification but also as a matter of personal identity. A person's role is not only his patterned way of evaluating and behaving toward the world of others; it is also his way of evaluating and behaving toward himself. In these terms all behavior is the reflection of a role, and all social interaction is a continuous sequence of interacting roles, or role-playing episodes; in these terms all the world is a stage, and all the men and women are actors.

Learning for Social Interaction

The process of human socialization, of learning and playing a role, begins as the infant grows out of total immersion in the world of physical feelings, of biological needs and satisfactions. He slowly becomes aware of others and learns to differentiate people and groups of people, as mother from father, parents from more distant others. As he learns to distinguish frowns from smiles, no from yes, he enters the world of meaning that lies behind the symbolism of gestures and words; he thus takes the first steps toward socialization into the human community.

The communications from the people about him, beginning with simple signs of approval and disapproval, love and rejection, become of great importance to the young child. From their attitudes toward him, expressed as words and gestures, he is able to verify his feelings about the world; he begins to understand and measure himself, his environment, and the relation between himself and his environment. Cooley describes a concept of "the looking glass self," wherein the child comes to see and know himself through the eyes of others, as though his characteristics and worth are reflected in the ways other people behave toward him.[12] He also becomes aware of the relative significance to him of different people and groups and learns to vary his interactions accordingly, responding to a parent more emphatically than to a casual visitor.[19]

As the child grows into an adult this process of gathering information and interacting becomes increasingly meaningful and complex. He learns to behave differently with close friends than with less important others, with his wife than with his colleagues. How he interacts with other people is determined by (1) his feelings about other people, (2) his perceptions of their feelings and behaviors toward him, and (3) his own feelings about himself, derived from these perceptions. The nature of his interactions affects, in turn, his feelings and perceptions of others and of himself. Thus the individual is involved in cyclic actions: his role is developed and continuously reevaluated by his interactions with others; his interactions with others are partly determined by this role.

The Role of the Other

The human being, then, perceives how people feel about him by interpreting their behavior, expressed in actions or words, and assigning meanings to it. These meanings may make him feel good or bad, wanted or unwanted, respected or disrespected. From this perception he forms a systematic understanding of the situation and of his role in it. For example, if a teacher sees that he is snubbed by his principal, he may be puzzled or take offense, or he may assume that the principal is in a bad mood. If he finds, however, that the principal continues to snub him day after day but responds cordially to other teachers, he may then conclude that the principal dislikes him. Thus the same act, the snubbing, has come to have a new meaning for the teacher as the circumstances have changed with time.

However, one of the commonest causes of interpersonal conflict is the misinterpretation of another's behavior. The teacher may be wrong in his interpretation: the principal may not be expressing a real dislike of the teacher but merely a disapproval of certain of his actions that he does not want or know how to discuss with him. On the other hand, the principal may actually be unaware of his behavior or of its effect on the teacher. The accuracy of a person's interpretations depends on a number of factors, some personal or psychological, others situational or environmental. A primary factor is how well he knows the person whose behavior he is trying to interpret. With increased familiarity he can begin to understand more accurately the meanings intended in the other's physical and verbal messages.

As important as personal contacts is the common recognition of meanings assigned to certain words and deeds. Different cultures and sub-cultures, as well as individuals, use and interpret words and gestures differently. Thus the smile, the handshake, and verbal teasing are symptoms of warm and friendly feelings between persons in most of the American culture. But the lower-class adolescent is more likely to tease physically than verbally, and the Frenchman may kiss his neighbor's cheek rather than shake his hand.

To recognize either common or shared meanings implicit in another's behavior, a person must be able to put himself in the other's place and attempt to appreciate the other's feelings and thoughts by (1) imagining the characteristics of the other's role and (2) engaging in the other's typical interaction with a new set of others, including himself. "How would I feel if that had happened to me?" "What would I mean if I'd said that?" or "What does he mean by that?" are questions by which one may begin to approach the role of the other. When one is able to answer such questions as "How does he feel about what I did?" "What will he do now that I've said what I did?" or "What does he think I really meant?" he has assumed the other's role; he is looking at and measuring himself from the vantage point of a different understanding of, and relation to, the world. He may be surprised at what he sees and answers.

Once he is able to step into, and act upon, another's role, and to see himself as others see him, a person may attain a clearer understanding of how he affects other people and why they behave toward him as they do. From having been able to play the other's role, he may have become aware of his own role as he might never have been conscious of it before. With this awareness, he may be able to effect changes in his role that can improve the nature of his social interaction and his feelings about himself and others.

The classroom offers good examples of interaction among people based on assumptions regarding the role that each is expected to play. The child has a good idea of how his teacher is likely to behave, since

7

he has had much prior experience with teachers. As the child gains more knowledge of his teacher, he can modify some of his role expectations and fairly accurately predict that teacher's behavior. Should the teacher behave in a way inconsistent with these expectations and predictions of his role, the student is very likely to be confused or frustrated.

The student also has some clear notions about his own role as a student. These self-expectations have developed out of his past experience as a student, through interaction with his present teacher, and through observation of and interaction with other students. Peers will often encourage or constrain a student to act a certain way in class, thus expressing their concern with appropriate role behavior.

The teacher, who has learned his role through a long period of professional training and experience, also has expectations about the way the students will and should interact with each other and with him. When students "get out of line," "don't show proper respect for the teacher," or "are disorderly," he knows that they are behaving in ways that will disrupt or threaten the fairly well-established and anticipated role relations of the classroom. It is clear that all these roles are in part determined by the nature of the institution in which they operate; adult-youth interaction that is appropriate in the grocery store or on the athletic field may not be appropriate in the classroom.

A role, then, is a patterned sequence of feelings, words, and actions, however indistinct this pattern may seem in the complexity of life situations. The process of getting information about the effects of one's role behavior is called feedback. The examples of role behavior and feedback given above are far more simplified than they usually are in everyday life, where fewer controls on social situations and the greater complexity of interaction usually prevent the definition of such clear-cut patterns of behavior. The fewer the formal standards of behavior and the less structured the situation, the greater the variety of behaviors that will ensue and the more informal and vague will be the feedback process. But despite its frequent lack of clarity, daily life does involve the same principles and sequence as the simplified examples we have discussed: perceiving and interpreting the actions of others; acting upon the interpretation; getting feedback as to the appropriateness of this behavior; and making further behavioral corrections.

One way to develop an understanding of oneself and of others is through an open and public discussion of the rules of behavior and their violation. Through such discussion, children and adults can learn about personal and social standards or expectations of behavior; they can inquire into the motivations for behavior, why certain people behave as they do. An ability to understand or appreciate the feelings of others can be gained also by imitating their behavior and examining how one felt when acting the other's role. Children often imitate the behavior of their peers and parents; they often adopt the seemingly successful ways in which their models have adapted to the world.[20] What needs to be added to this natural imitative process is a conscious awareness that it is being done and the time, energy, and ability to discuss its implications. The natural imitative and dramatic abilities of children can be translated into a systematic and fruitful educational experience if such awareness and discussion are made available to them.

Role Playing to Improve Interpersonal Relations

If skill in understanding the feelings, thoughts, and role of the other is essential for a successful interpretation of events and relations, then an instructional tool that provides such experiences should be very helpful. Role playing is a method of instruction that meets these needs; individuals take on the roles of other people and act out the others' feelings, thoughts, and behavior.

The success of role playing in the improvement of social relations has been amply demonstrated in several institutional settings. The experience of industrial training programs in changing workers' perceptions and attitudes is one example. Maier has described the effects of role-playing techniques in the following way:

"In experiencing the role-playing process one learns to pay attention to what is done, and it is through increased attention to detail that one improves with practice. It is a general principle in the acquisition of skill that improvement takes place only through conscious effort during performance. . . . Role playing readily demonstrates that hostility, threats and suspicion stimulate hostile and defensive reactions in others, whereas generosity, tolerance and desire to see another's point of view stimulate constructive and social behavior in him. It is in experiencing these relationships in reality practice that they can become practical living principles."[17]

In the same report Maier describes several role-playing situations that would be effective components of a successful human-relations training program in industry. Many such techniques are currently being incorporated into training sessions for foremen, managers, and union leaders; all aim toward the improvement of industrial practice through the improvement of relations between people.

Many trained psychologists use role playing or modified forms of role playing as part of the therapeutic process. Moreno, in particular, is a pioneer therapist and author in this field who directs a series of dramatic

9

workshops in individual and group therapy. In a process that he calls psychodrama, Moreno's patients act out real-life situations, and are asked to discuss their individual insights.[6] Such public enactment of a personal problem, with the director and audience helping the patient by adding their reactions to the information that the patient has already gained, often helps the individual to see his behavior through the eyes of others. It thereby provides a type of feedback that may help the person change his behavior.

Some studies of role behavior focus attention on how situations differ according to the point of view of the participant. For instance, the teacher and the student can observe the same event, yet form different interpretations and conclusions. In an attempt to understand this phenomenon, Rosenberg studied the effect of a role-playing situation upon the participants, identifiers, and observers. She notes not only that the dramatic situation influences the actors themselves, but also that the involved or noninvolved audience can benefit from the role-playing experience. Rosenberg states:

"In general the participants are highly emotional about the scene and keenly aware of the feelings and emotions of others within the scene. . . . Observers are . . . extremely general in their report of what has happened but are not aware of the feelings and emotions involved. . . . Identifiers, although emotionally involved, tend to be extremely critical."[22]

If we think of *participants* as actors in a situation, *observers* as noninvolved outsiders, and *identifiers* as people who attempt to link themselves emotionally with one of the participants, we can see how this description of the role-playing situation correlates with everyday life. These various degrees and modes of an individual's emotional involvement in a situation are key factors in interpreting his reaction to that situation.

In discussing other hypotheses about role-playing abilities, Dymond states:

"The ability to feel and describe the thoughts and feelings of others (empathy) is accompanied by a better understanding of the relationships one has with others (insight). Conversely, those who are less able to take the role of the other seem also to lack insight into their own interpersonal relations."[13]

Here again appears the intimate connection between the two essential components of successful social interaction: an ability to understand the thoughts and feelings of other persons and an understanding of oneself in relation to other people.[13, 16] It seems clear that role playing has proved to be an effective technique for the examination of, and instruction in, some of these critical skills.

Role Playing to Understand Social Problems

The social relationships of the individual extend beyond his direct interpersonal contacts with other people. He is a member of various social groups, which in turn relate to other groups. Many of the human-relations problems of the American society stem in part from expressions of group attitudes and feelings. A social class, an ethnic group, a club, a gang—these develop norms of thinking and behaving that affect the individual member and his relation to people within and outside the group.

Social problems of minority groups, juvenile delinquency, corruption in government, prejudice, political behavior, and international relations involve relationships between the individual and the group. If the individual concerned is to understand such issues and devise intelligent courses of action, he needs insight into the kinds of group norms and social pressures operating in his particular situation.

Role playing has been found to be a very useful technique in this area. In college courses and adult study groups dealing with international problems, members have taken the roles of some of the principals in an international dispute in order to gain insights into the forces involved. For example, one group acts the roles of the Russian delegate and his advisers at a disarmament conference; another takes the roles of the representatives of a nonaligned country such as India. Having to represent these points of view realistically at the conference table helps the participants to cut through some of the stereotypes to which propaganda has conditioned their thinking. In this use of role playing—as a study technique—group rather than individual relationships are involved.

Thus the opportunity to place oneself in a position to see the situation as others see it—and, moreover, to be responsible for behaving as the other person or persons would behave—may help one develop insights and understanding that might not be reached through traditional educational methods.

The classroom itself is a life experience in which the students engage in social interaction, from the rudimentary forms in the earliest grades to the more sophisticated and purposeful forms of the young adult. Skill in these behavior patterns is important in the student's relation to his work, his peers, and his teachers—indeed, in his entire development as a human being. Since role playing has been suggested as a technique for teaching, clarifying, and practicing such skills, it is appropriate to examine some of the objectives and ways of using role playing in the classroom.

CHAPTER THREE

Role Playing in the Classroom

During their recent studies dealing with the process of identification and diffusion of innovative teaching practices, the authors discovered many classroom teachers experimenting with role playing. They were using it as a method for teaching children to look at themselves, to look at the actions and behaviors of others, and to look at social life in general. They were using it to help in the diagnosis and treatment of classroom interpersonal problems, for teaching lessons in interpersonal relations, and to give feedback and insights to particular individuals. They were using it to dramatize and illustrate subject matter in courses such as history and English. They were using it, in short, as a means of making the classroom a real-life laboratory for social and academic learning.

Role Playing and Learning

Role playing has a tremendous potential for the average elementary and secondary school classroom.

First, by taking on the role of another person and by pretending to feel like, think like, and act like another person, students can act out their true feelings without the risk of sanctions or reprisals. They know they are only acting, and can thus express feelings ordinarily kept hidden. This experience can give rise to greater individual spontaneity and creativity in previously repressed or inhibited children.

Second, students can examine and discuss relatively private issues and problems without anxiety. These problems are not focused on the self; they are attributed to a given role or stereotype. Thus children can avoid the normal anxiety accompanying the presentation of personal matters that may violate rules and regulations. This experience may result in greater individual insights into behavior and a better understanding of the place of rules and behaviorial standards. Such learning can best be accomplished in a nonjudgmental situation where "correct" solutions are not the goal.

Third, by placing themselves in the role of another, students can identify with the real worlds and the imaginations of other children and adults. In this manner they may begin to understand the effects of their behavior on others, and they may gain significant information about the motivations for their own and other people's behaviors. By sympathizing with the scapegoat, many a bully may understand how it feels to be picked on; by sympathizing with the bully, many a scapegoat may understand why his behavior is a red flag to the bully. When both roles are examined and discussed by the entire class, both bully and scapegoat may understand how their behavior looks to others, what some of their needs or motivations are, and what other forms of action might be appropriate. Students can begin to develop an elementary but systematic understanding of the science of human relations from repeated experiences and discussions of this sort.

Fourth, this increased opportunity for understanding oneself and others paves the way for behavioral change. Achieving systematic insights into self, into others, and into motivations for various actions can aid students in clarifying their own values and in effectively directing or changing their own behavior. By practicing a variety of behaviors in a series of role-playing exercises and by discussing the effects of each, students may be able to make more realistic choices for their actions than before. The supportive atmosphere may also legitimize in the students' eyes the peer-helping process in the classroom, encouraging them to give and receive insights, suggestions, and help.

Fifth, role playing may also be used to demonstrate less personal but pervasive problems between and among people and groups. Social problems, to the extent that they reflect conflict between man and man, can be dramatized fruitfully in the classroom. For instance, classroom portrayals of problems of prejudice may lead to greater understanding of the dynamics of this phenomenon and some clarification of ways of dealing with its occurrence. Such understanding need not be purely abstract, on the theoretical or moralistic level; it can include the alternative behaviors that are available when one is a witness to an act or feeling of racial, religious, or economic bias. Further, small-scale examples of political events, instances of political decision making, or dilemmas facing criminals and courts of law can be examined in the classroom. These portrayals may help make the student aware of selected social problems and the human

13

meaning for those involved. They may help him to examine thoughtfully different ways of resolving social and personal conflict and to identify the advantages and disadvantages of each path. The exercises may not reduce conflict, but they may give the student skills to deal with his world more effectively. He may come to see the ways in which some of these universal social issues are reflected in his own relations with other individuals and groups and how they bear upon the decisions he must make in his own life.

Sixth, role playing that helps individuals to understand their own and others' behaviors can free them to utilize their intellectual potential more fully. Substantial research has shown that interpersonal relations and feelings of high or low self-esteem affect a student's academic performance. Thus role playing directed toward understanding and changing interpersonal situations may lead indirectly to a higher level of academic performance. But it may also be used to present academic materials. Historical or contemporary events can be acted out in class to dramatize the feelings and conflicts of the participants in pivotal situations. After a brief introduction to the plot and characters, students can role-play a story, a novel, or a play in English class. The comparison between the student's portrayal and the author's presentation may stimulate thoughtful discussions about the author's style and point of view, the historical context and traditions, and similar topics. The technique of role playing can bring to the study of academic materials the dramatic import, the immediacy, and the student involvement that may otherwise be lacking in the classroom.

Seventh, role playing may prove to be an instructional technique particularly useful with nonverbal, acting-out students. The typical middle-class child is apt to be satisfied with intellectual talk about a problem but reluctant to express the feelings and emotions necessary to a full understanding of the dynamics of the problem situation, or hesitant to carry his talk into action. Lower-class students, on the other hand, often reject the verbalism and abstraction of many school activities, but delight in giving their more visceral responses. Through the acting-out technique of role playing, lower-class students can have a chance to experience success by making a valued contribution to the class activity in a way that is within their range of skills, and they can thereby become more highly involved in the total learning activity. Middle-class students, through the confrontation with feelings and action provided by role playing, may learn to express concretely their intellectual understandings.

A final and unique advantage of role playing as an instructional technique is its active nature. Participants and audiences do not merely discuss theoretical problems of behavior and alternative ways of acting; they observe and practice new ways of behaving. Thus there is a stress on active participation in learning that enhances the learning itself. The necessary connection is made between knowing a principle and acting upon that knowledge. The mere addition of information neither solves classroom interpersonal problems nor teaches new social relations: interpersonal issues are resolved only as students or teachers begin to behave differently. New behavior is the testimony of new information; it changes the effects one person has upon other persons. The shy child who can intellectually appreciate the importance of taking the initiative in beginning a conversation may practice this insight through role playing. With successful dramatic experience under his belt, he may be better able to introduce these new behaviors into the real-life situation. Similarly, the bully who has come to understand himself and the scapegoat through observation and discussion has an opportunity to practice alternative ways of dealing with his aggressive feelings.

Skill practice in role playing is only one step in this change process, but through such understanding and practice and with decreased anxiety and isolation, a student may become willing and able to take the additional steps to change. He may still require a great deal of practice and reinforcement before he can apply these lessons to his own experience and actually perform more effectively.

Thus role playing can be seen as one technique in an educational procedure that is directed toward the scientific improvement of classroom learning and social behavior. Such a procedure assumes that learning needs to be more than "studying about" and more than mere activity or "real-life experiences." The classroom can provide the opportunities for relating ideas to action, theory to practice. It can become a laboratory for problem identification, for experience and analysis, for drawing conclusions, for formulating and reality-testing new behaviors, and for learning to generalize and behave differently in other situations.

The Boundaries of Classroom Role Playing

The preceding chapter discussed different uses of role playing—industrial and psychotherapeutic as well as educational. There are also several depths or levels at which role playing can be used within a single program. The uses with students range from classroom instruction and portrayal of literary or historical events, through examination of individual and group problems in social skill development, to intensive personal or group psychotherapy with disturbed students.

The classroom teacher need not be a psychologist to use role playing at the instructional and interpersonal levels. In general, the kinds of problems he chooses to work with can and should be dealt with as "sociodramas": that is, with emphasis on typical roles, problems, or situations that children usually face. For example, the teacher may wish to portray

15

such stereotypes as the "shy child," the child "dealing with aggression" or "learning how to use the resources of adults." These are conditions in which students must learn appropriate and effective roles. As such, they are excellent examples of topics for role playing.

The teacher can avoid too direct a confrontation of any individual student by concentrating on such roles, or typical behavior patterns. The application of general problems to a specific student's abilities or inabilities should be initiated primarily by the student as a result of whatever insights he has developed. A respect for the student's ability to deal effectively with new information is a help at this point. The teacher should not engage in depth probing, nor should he publicly air a reluctant individual's problems. A basic rule is that the teacher should be cautious of involving himself and his students in portrayals and interpretations that seriously impinge upon their psychological privacy or security. Psychodrama and other intensive and individualized forms of role playing are ordinarily used for therapeutic purposes and should be attempted only by the trained therapist. The potential dangers of an overzealous confrontation of a disturbed or even a seemingly healthy child by an untrained technician are well worth these precautions and limitations.

Within these limitations, however, even the relatively inexperienced teacher can learn to use role playing effectively. Starting with a simple charade, a short problem story, or other relatively "safe" topics, a teacher can experiment with increasingly complex and meaningful issues dependent upon his own skill, confidence, and specialized training. As the students and teacher continue to practice, classroom rapport and acceptance are likely to grow. Within such a supportive atmosphere individual students are likely to become more comfortable about discussing their insights, accepting suggestions, and changing their behaviors.

Increased freedom of emotional expression, involvement in and portrayal of a role that is not one's own, and the dramatic presentation of lifelike events are as much a part of the role-playing technique as they are of acting and creative dramatics. Role playing, however, does not regard the development of dramatic skills as ends in themselves. It seeks to utilize whatever abilities a child may have in these areas as tools with which to influence his social and academic growth. The improvisation and public discussion of dramatic presentations are strategies for leading the classroom group toward greater learning and change.

Classroom Needs and Role-Playing Strategies

The role-playing technique should not be used as an isolated classroom event or experience. Like any good educational tool, it is best used as part of a larger instructional plan. Any particular role-playing situation must be selected and adapted on the basis of the teacher's professional judgment as he diagnoses and assesses the educational needs of his classroom. The teacher's decision as to how and when to use this technique is crucial to effective learning.*

The issue or problem to be enacted in class may be a real-life situation or a fictitious example of a real situation. Role-playing situations may develop from interpersonal problems in the classroom, from outside issues facing young people, or from the desire to present subject matter more forcefully and dramatically. In any case, the problem situation should be concrete and real enough for students to understand its relevance to their daily lives.

One way of getting relevance is to provide for student involvement and participation in planning the role-playing exercises. The teacher might simply ask the class to suggest personal or general problems that they think can be studied. Alternatively, he might take a problem census by asking his students to list some common problem situations they have experienced. After his students have some experience with the technique, the teacher will generally find them eagerly suggesting new situations or events with which to role-play. The teacher who has clarified his own learning goals, and who has carefully diagnosed and interpreted the social situation in his classroom, is in an advantageous position to construct a drama designed to deal with those issues especially relevant to his students.

Once a diagnosis is made and a problem situation selected, some other guidelines are important. The topic or problem should be clear, specific, and not too complex. It should be a topic that can be handled, solved, or investigated by the group members without making them feel inadequate. Both teacher and students will improve in their role-playing skill as they have common positive experiences, but too much should not be tried too early. Tense and emotionally threatening situations should not be used initially with a class new to reflecting on its own behavior with the role-playing technique. At some point threatening issues are necessary and important to deal with, since they often represent the areas of greatest growth potential. But comfort with this content and learning style develops gradually, and episodes that are threatening to the teacher or his students should be avoided until the class has developed positive ways of handling feelings.

*For a discussion of the importance of this diagnostic process in solving classroom problems, see Schmuck, Chesler, and Lippitt, *Problem Solving to Improve Classroom Learning* (Chicago: Science Research Associates, 1966). Detailed examples of tools for diagnosing many types of classroom problems, including instructions for their selection, administration, and interpretation, are presented in Fox, Luszki, and Schmuck, *Diagnosing Classroom Learning Environments* (Chicago: Science Research Associates, 1966).

A decision to use role playing for dealing with controversial problems in which parents and the community, as well as the students, are deeply involved requires careful consideration and evaluation. Race relations, sex, religion, moral values, politics, cultural conflicts, parent-child relations—these areas may provide educational topics of impelling urgency and relevance. Through role playing, young people can examine some of their true feelings in a nonthreatening atmosphere, explore possible consequences of alternative actions, and derive some help in facing these problems constructively. The degree to which the student can and should be exposed to these problems will vary with each classroom.

Controversial problems can be dealt with at several levels of abstraction or immediacy. One approach avoids facing such issues directly, but offers the student opportunities to experience, observe, and think about different ways of reacting to situations pertinent to his life as a student and a human being in a social context. Role playing allows the student to experience success in such general areas as interpersonal communication and to try out ways of dealing with problems of human relationships. The gratification, confidence, and insight into motives that the student gains from acting out roles with his peers can open up new alternatives and provide new skills for dealing with more controversial situations as they arise outside the classroom. Many teachers who have been working conscientiously with the problems of disadvantaged youth and minority groups are convinced that the most fruitful results are obtained by giving these students some experience with success, rather than a further reflection of the constant demoralization and defeat they face in their lives out of school.

Another approach faces controversial problems more directly but presents them in a generalized form: "What do you say when your dad refuses to let you have the car for a date at the drive-in movie?" "How can a girl respond graciously to a compliment from a boy?" "What can your class do when a new child from a minority group joins the class and some of your classmates are making things difficult for him?" This approach remains impersonal, does not single out particular individuals or groups, and is relatively nonthreatening. Many children may not yet have had personal experience with interracial, religious, or intimate interpersonal situations. Role playing helps them anticipate some of these problems in more meaningful ways than would mere discussion. It also provides a chance for those students who have realistic contacts with such situations to bring to bear their information and insights as resources rather than as evidence of personal difficulties. Opportunities like this are going to be increasingly needed if youth living in the somewhat restricted environment provided by each community (no matter how "privileged" it may be) are to become alert to, and learn to deal at least in an elementary way with the human-relations problems of a complex urban society.

A more direct approach may be made to specific incidents or problems in interpersonal relations as they arise. As the teacher and class become skilled and comfortable with role playing, this is perhaps the most rewarding technique of all. If used with nonthreatening problems, such as testing how a new child is to be greeted by the others, or how to appreciate a new passage in English literature, the teacher can have the class play an actual incident by assigning roles quickly and informally. Much greater care needs to be exercised in more sensitive situations such as race relations or sexual behavior. The teacher needs to have an established rapport with parents, a supportive working relationship with his principal, and, most important of all, the confidence of his students. Given such conditions, role playing is a means for students to deal with difficult issues, which are *already a vital part of their living,* in an accepting and educationally planned atmosphere, guided by an understanding and expert adult.

Another issue in role-playing strategy involves the length of a program or session. Very young children usually enjoy a session of not longer than fifteen to twenty minutes. Older elementary school children may stay highly involved for twenty to thirty minutes; junior and senior high school students forty-five minutes or more. These times include, of course, the relevant preparation, discussion, and evaluation activities. The actual role-playing improvisations are likely to last only a few minutes before they are cut for analysis, discussion, and reenactment.

Finally, it may be pointed out that a well-planned curriculum unit for interpersonal learning frees the teacher from complete dependence on incidental or accidental problem situations, which might cause overwhelming strategic and organizational problems. However, too rigorous advance planning may overlook the learning potential in immediate events or problems. A good balance of planned and spontaneous activities, oriented to meeting educational goals, may be the best strategy for the teacher. Some teachers set aside a regular weekly period that the class comes to anticipate as the time to consider a variety of topics and problems for role playing. Other teachers utilize role playing when the opportunity presents itself as a part of the continuing class activity, rather than on any regular basis. With either strategy, role playing is most effective when used in conjunction with specifically planned educational goals and procedures.

The Teacher's Self-preparation

The effective use of an instructional tool depends upon the teacher's knowledge of it and his assurance in using it. The first time he threads a motion picture projector, even after reading the directions carefully, he may be awkward and slow. Since this is embarrassing with a class impatient to see the picture, most teachers practice a bit in private or have the projector threaded and ready to go before the pupils come into the room.

It is not so simple to prepare oneself for role playing. Practice cannot be accomplished in private; interaction with other persons is needed to develop skills and confidence in the technique. Many teachers might be reluctant to try role playing without a clear conception of what their specific job is and without a series of practice runs. As one teacher put it:

> "I've read some material about role playing. I'm interested in the possibilities it might hold for my classroom. But what do I do? How can I keep from falling flat on my face and having my class in chaos? How do I get started?"

It is understandable that there may be some initial fear or reluctance to introducing role playing into the classroom. Many teachers fear that spontaneity in the classroom will lead to a loss of control or chaos, and many attempt to avoid all show of emotion in the class for this reason. Teachers subject to such fears are apt to be those unfamiliar with the technique, new teachers without an instructional plan, or experienced teachers who are relatively set in their ways. However, emotional factors do influence learning and a temporary loss of unilateral teacher control may not mean chaos or permanent loss of influence. Several suggestions for meeting the initial problems of getting started may be helpful.

A first step might be practicing or exploring the technique with a few other people—with friends, family, or colleagues. Perhaps several other teachers in a school would also like to get the feel of role playing and would agree to meet after school or in the evening. Some of the situations suggested in the Appendix could be tried, with each teacher taking turns at being the director and playing the various roles. It would be ideal, of course, to secure the consultant help of some teacher who has used role playing and is willing to share some of his experience. Failing this, or in addition, the advice of recognized experts or other resource persons might be sought.

In one instance the authors set up an actual session to instruct teachers in the administration of role playing to their classes. It focused on a common teacher problem—teacher interaction. The report of this session states:

> "The next training session, on role playing, was most successful. The locale of the role-play situation was designated as the teachers' lunchroom where several teachers had gathered and one teacher was to present ideas for a new curriculum outline to the others. In the design we included a hostile colleague, a pair of close friends, a 'principal

worrier,' a discussion blocker, and two teachers who would immediately support the ideas. Some teachers were a little anxious from the beginning and did not wish to participate; they were made observers whose job it was to report objectively on what happened.

"We went ahead and got thoroughly embroiled—the hostile colleague, in particular, doing a good job. We noted, during the play, a previously hidden staff resentment of the principal's role and some antagonistic staff alignments. The participants recognized some of these issues and accepted them as problems of role relationships, not as problems of individual personalities or abilities. They will probably be able to understand and improve staff relations as a result. After the role play was completed, we moved to a discussion of how this technique might be used to deal with students' feelings in the classroom."

In this adult session the role-playing exercise was most helpful in bringing previously hidden problems to the surface, in allowing teachers to understand how it feels to innovate or to suggest innovation in a crowded lunchroom, and in giving the participants some skill in planning and administering role playing.

A second step in self-preparation might be to interest a small group of students in staying after school to try out some "creative dramatics." These few class members can be taken into the teacher's confidence, and learning this new technique can be made a cooperative project in which the teacher admits that he has not used it with a class before and is experimenting. The students can help by trying out some role-playing episodes as well as suggesting what can be done in class to improve the sessions. In class the teacher and his helpers can explain their collaboration in the development of this teaching-learning technique.

As suggested earlier, the teacher using role playing for the first time should start with very simple situations that are familiar to the students and in which the action is clear-cut—for instance, "Your best friend, Jane, asks you to her birthday party when you have a date. What do you say?" Other simple examples are listed in the early parts of the Appendix. Later the students and teacher can move to more difficult problems. The early periods should be brief and should be stopped while student interest is still high. It it not necessary for every student to be an actor in the first role-playing session.

In preparing for a role-playing session, the teacher may find it helpful to write out briefing sheets to give or read to each participant in the improvisation. Examples of these instructions are shown in Chapter Five. He may also feel more secure at first by writing out ahead of time a detailed description of the situation and of the instructions to the audience. As he

21

becomes sufficiently confident to introduce on-the-spot improvisations, he will become more facile in extemporizing the situations and instructions.

As a general rule, and particularly in the early sessions, the teacher and the students should talk over how each session went. The teacher should solicit student help in searching for reasons why the role playing did not work as well as it might have. Such student involvement results in more effective learning and focuses responsibility for improvement of role playing on the class and teacher together, rather than on the teacher alone.

Steps in the Role-Playing Sequence

Role playing in the classroom works best when there is an attempt to follow a definite sequence of steps. The sequence outlined below allows for a logical ordering and development of the role-playing session. It has been tested successfully by teachers.

Preparation and instruction, the first stage, covers problem selection, warm-up, and general and specific instructions to participants and audience. It involves the selection by the teacher, with or without class help, of an issue or problem to be worked on. After selecting the problem, the teacher needs to warm up or relax the students and give them practice and security in public performance and expression. The explanation of the general problem situation should make clear the educational purposes of the drama and the relevance of the issue or problem for the entire class. The teacher is now ready to brief the actors, to explain in detail the exact role each of them will play. The final step in this stage is to delineate the roles of the audience, the students who are not acting out the dramatic roles. These students can observe the general interaction of actors, or they can be charged to watch for specific actors or for specific events.

Dramatic action and discussion, the second major stage, covers both the role playing itself and the subsequent discussion and interpretation of the action. Sufficient time should be allowed during the improvisation for students to become thoroughly immersed in the problem situation, so that they can take full advantage of the situation's promise for discovering and practicing alternative ways of acting. At the conclusion of the drama it is important to bring the class back to everyday reality, to dissociate the actors clearly from the role they played. This is important so that critics and other students can concentrate on the role behavior and not on the actions or person of the actors. The post-role-playing discussion may take several forms and involve several different students or groups of students. The role players or the audience, or both, may contribute to an analysis of the dramatic session. A final important focus of this learning experience should be the student's ability to apply the examples and lessons of this new role behavior to his own interpersonal experiences.

Evaluation, the final stage, must follow the enactment and discussion of the role-playing situation. In this stage the teacher and pupils review the successes and failures of their role-playing experience. The purposes, procedures, and effects of such a learning experience should be analyzed so that teacher and class can make decisions about the need for additional role playing or reenactment of the scene. The teacher will certainly want to make a further personal evaluation of the experience in the light of his original diagnosis and goals; he will want to consider what verbal and behavioral evidence there is to show that the students have learned from the experience.

CHAPTER FOUR

Case Studies in the Use of Role Playing

Two examples, or case studies, of role playing as used by classroom teachers are presented in this chapter. They demonstrate how the sequence of steps described in Chapter Three can be applied in the classroom situation. Chapter Eight will present several more case studies after the intervening chapters have offered detailed suggestions on how to implement each of the various steps.

A Study of Intergrade Rivalry and Aggression

The first case is from Mrs. Adams' fourth-grade classroom. The dialogue of the improvisation was quoted in the opening pages of this booklet.

1. *Selecting the role-playing problem.* Mrs. Adams decided to work with intergrade rivalry and aggression because it seemed to be a recurrent schoolyard and neighborhood problem. Her students were frequently involved in arguments and fights with older children. Moreover, the students had expressed the desire to have training in how to deal with siblings. These closely connected issues convinced Mrs. Adams that the problem was important to her students.

2. *Warm-up.* Mrs. Adams' class had considerable role-playing experience; therefore she decided to omit any warm-up.

3. *Explaining the general situation.* Prior to the reported dialogue the teacher and her students had discussed briefly the kinds of problems members of the class were having with older children. Mrs. Adams then explained the general problem situation to the entire class:

> We've been talking about problems that boys and girls have in getting along with others who are a few years older or younger than they are. Today, let's see if we can show what might happen to cause problems between fourth-grade students and sixth-graders. (*She places a chair in front of the room.*)
>
> Let's pretend that this (*pointing to the chair*) is a hill. It's been snowing for a couple of days, and many boys and girls like to come here with their sleds. Now suppose there are two fourth-graders sledding. They have only one sled, so they've been riding double. They have just run into a rock which has bent the runner so that the sled doesn't work. They try to fix it—to bend it back into shape—but they can't. Then they see two sixth-graders coming over the hill. Each sixth-grader has a new sled that he is eager to try out.
>
> One of the fourth-graders thinks she should ask the sixth-grader for help; the other one isn't sure the older children will help. He doesn't see any point in asking, but the first one decides to ask for help anyway.

Mrs. Adams had now stated the real-life problem, set the geographic and climatic conditions surrounding the exercise, and suggested how the action might be started. The entire class has been briefed on the action that might take place.

4. *Explaining participant roles.* Mrs. Adams cast the scene and instructed the players about their roles.

> Let's see what would happen. Who would like to be a fourth-grader? . . . All right, Danny and Linda will be the fourth-graders. How about some sixth-graders? . . . All right, Leon and Gwen, you are the sixth-graders. Fine. . . .
>
> Let's start the skit, Danny and Linda, with your being two typical fourth-graders named Fred and Florence. You are talking with each other before the sixth-graders appear. Come on up to the front of the room on this "hill." Leon and Gwen, you are two sixth-graders named Stan and Susan, and you come over to the hill later.

These four roles were all quite simple, so there was little need for detailed instruction. There was little formal structuring of roles, so that the actors were permitted a wide latitude of possible behaviors. In the event she wanted to use more complex, lengthy, or structured roles, Mrs. Adams might have written out the instructions and handed them to each participant. In this example she asked for volunteers to play certain roles and made no attempt to assign particular students to particular roles. This procedure, again, was possible because of her class's prior experience in role playing. In other circumstances Mrs. Adams might not have selected certain volunteers or might have suggested other children for these roles.

5. *Explaining audience roles.* Mrs. Adams' instructions to the re-mainder of the class were general and did not demand a very active role of them.

The class members who do not have parts will be the audience. You should watch the actors carefully to see if they play their parts as you think boys and girls you know would actually behave. Think about what other things they could do to solve their problems.

The nonplayers were to observe the role-playing process: to examine the content of the problem itself and to evaluate the manner in which the role players solved this problem. The class's reactions could then be used in the discussion period to augment information from the actors regarding their feelings and actions during the dramatic session.

6. *The role playing.* In the improvisations Mrs. Adams permitted the players to initiate the argument on their own, and she did not cut into or call an end to the scene until the conflict had been concluded. In earlier sessions, however, Mrs. Adams had had to intervene often to stimulate dialogue. She had experienced no situations that were intoler-able in terms of hostile or disruptive performance; her interventions were necessary only to help children who were reluctant to enter into a dialogue appropriate to the role-playing session. This aid had taken the form of "How would you respond to that?" or "Ask him why he did that." With this prompting, the children were usually able to continue the session themselves.

7. *Discussion.* In the discussion after the role-playing session, the class concentrated on first one and then another of the participant roles. Mrs. Adams asked the class how they thought the fourth-graders in the scene felt about the way things turned out. The class observed that the fourth-graders felt "sorry," "jealous," "mad," "angry." Some members of the class suggested alternative behaviors for the fourth-graders: "They should have said 'Please.'" "They should not have pushed Leon's sled."

"They should not have called names, but should have walked away." The sixth-graders were seen as wanting to "feel big," wanting "the hill for themselves," and as feeling the fourth-graders "were acting smart." Some explanations for why the role-playing interaction took the form it did were "The sixth-graders didn't want to be bothered with little kids" and "The sixth-graders are nice, but because their big brothers and sisters act that way toward them, they act that way toward the fourth-graders."

Mrs. Adams then asked the class whether any of these problems were like the ones the students had with their older and younger siblings. Finally the class discussed some alternatives to cross-age and interclass rivalry and aggression. They suggested bringing in some sixth-graders as resource people to tell them what they didn't like about "little kids" and what might be done to improve. The class members wondered if they could help themselves become a little more skillful in relating to older children by devising a variety of role-playing situations between older and younger children. They decided to try out some of these alternative behaviors by further role playing later.

8. *Evaluation.* The role-playing experience was evaluated by Mrs. Adams after the children had an opportunity to replay the session several times. After a variety of alternative solutions had been attempted, she tried to discover what impact the role playing had had upon the students' thinking and their behavior. She used some sociometric devices and an evaluation instrument that asked students to give their solutions to several hypothetical problems involving interpersonal relationships. Her findings included the following evidences of student growth:

1. Students were able to suggest a greater variety of solutions for a given problem situation.

2. They were less inhibited and more able to respond to one another's problems in class.

3. They were better able to act out their feelings and examine them in class.

4. Children who had been socially ineffective began to learn more appropriate and effective social behavior.

5. Formerly rejected children were increasingly integrated into the classroom process.

6. The students asked her to arrange joint sessions with older classes so that the lessons of the role-playing experience could be shared with real sixth-graders.

Modifying Processes of Peer Criticism

This case is from the report of a sixth-grade teacher, Mrs. Breen, who had no prior experience with role playing but had read about it to gain a better understanding of the techniques. Because of the inexperience of the students, Mrs. Breen appropriately placed more emphasis on the selection and warm-up phases than did Mrs. Adams.

1. *Selecting the role-playing problem.* Mrs. Breen felt that her students were overly critical of their peers and that such criticism was working against the best interests of effective learning in her classroom. There was general grumbling and griping about individuals and minimal cooperation in work groups. Mrs. Breen felt that this classroom atmosphere could be changed if the children could see each other's actions from more than one point of view. She decided to focus, through role playing, on some of the situations that seemed to cause friction.

In accord with her plan, Mrs. Breen scheduled a class in "dramatics," in which the students were to construct their own short play. She reported on the class discussion of what the play should be about as follows:

> Should it be about home, children, school? I listed several plots on the board and advised the children to choose a plot that would be familiar to all of them. Then a question arose: What makes a plot interesting? It was seen that conflict, different points of view, and disagreements might be suitable elements to be included. The children refined their list to take these factors into account and ended this part of their preparation with the following recommendations as possible plots: an argument on the playground, disagreements between brothers and sisters, making a report to the class, and acting as a teacher taking charge of the class. They decided to try the playground situation first.

2. *Warm-up.* In warming up her students for the role-playing session, Mrs. Breen asked them to pretend that they had just won a ball game, and then that they had just lost. As the next step, she asked four students to come up to the front of the room, face the class, and act as if they were walking home on a cold day. Mrs. Breen continued with additional exercises of this sort until her students understood the difference between being oneself and acting like someone else, between actor and audience roles, and until many showed the ability and interest to perform in front of their classmates.

3. *Explaining the general situation.* The scene was to be the school-yard, where several boys and girls were competing in team sports. The main focus of the drama was on the reactions of the losing team. The children decided to characterize a braggart, a poor sport, and a person who is incompetent at sports but tries. Mrs. Breen introduced a new role, the diplomat, whose job was to mediate between the winners and the losers to minimize conflict. The children felt that these characterizations were sufficient for them to construct a spontaneous drama.

4. *Explaining participant roles.* The children decided that about half of the class should act in the drama and the other half should be the audience. Given the general situation described above, the students who were to play the drama were ready. There was absolutely no concern over who should play which part. Mrs. Breen permitted the drama to be played in this manner expecting that the results could be an important learning experience for both halves of the class.

5. *Explaining audience roles.* Mrs. Breen instructed the audience to watch how the different characters reacted in the playground situation, and to be prepared to make suggestions for improvement.

6. *The role playing.* Mrs. Breen reported, "The first cast tried it and bedlam followed. Reactions to the problem between the two teams were primarily physical; there was milling about and shoving. I stopped the action before an actual fight developed."

7. *Discussion.* The audience did not like the scene because people did not "say" anything. The physical reactions and mass confusion prevented the audience from following the action carefully and inhibited any attempts at experimenting with new behaviors. For instance, the diplomat never got an opportunity to smooth over the conflicts in the situation. The class evaluated how well each part was portrayed and how each, the diplomat in particular, could have been more effective. In addition, Mrs. Breen and the class talked about a variety of ways in which bad sportsmanship or unfair criticism might be handled.

8. *Reenactment.* After these discussions the same half of the class role-played again, and this time the audience felt it was much more successful. There was less physical confusion and more helpful discussion as a part of the scene. The diplomat was able to get his point of view across, and some of the characters experimented with new role behavior.

Later the same play was tried with the other half of the class. Eventually everyone in the class played the major roles at least once. The class noticed that each group and each individual performed the play a little differently, an observation that led to a penetrating and meaningful discussion of individual differences in student styles and backgrounds. This discussion explored why there might be a wide variety of alternative role responses in a given situation.

9. *Evaluation.* Mrs. Breen's observations about the effects of these role-playing sessions on behavior are very instructive.

Several days after experimenting with the first role-playing situation (the playground story) the class was challenged to a softball game by the other sixth grade. The girls played against the girls, the boys against the boys. The rules were very carefully observed. The class lost both games by narrow margins. As the girls came back to the room I heard some of the same comments that had been made by the actors during the role playing. The girls recognized these attitudes too and commented, "What are you, the poor sport?" and "Oh, you're just being the diplomat." Once these and other remarks had been made, everyone settled down and recovered very quickly from feelings of defeat. I heard no direct evidence from the boys, but when they came in they seemed to be normal. There was very little evidence of bad feeling about the losses.

In the example of role playing tried by Mrs. Breen, the children picked their own characters and structured the dramatic process themselves. At first this procedure seemed to create considerable confusion, but classroom discussion and teacher advice ironed out these problems fairly quickly. The situations and problems the children suggested seemed to be appropriate to their own needs and interests, and Mrs. Breen was pleased with their choice of issues. She planned multiple enactments of the role-playing situation and several discussion periods following each enactment. The results seemed to indicate that children were better able to deal with schoolyard competition and conflict because of their role-playing experience. Certain individuals, in fact, were able to develop alternative and more effective means of expressing their feelings.

CHAPTER FIVE

The Technique of Role Playing: Preparation and Instruction

The preceding chapter described how two teachers followed a sequence of steps in the use of role playing in the classroom. In this chapter the first stage, preparation and instruction, is examined in detail. The following specific steps occur in this stage: selecting the role-playing problem; warm-up; explaining the general situation; selecting the participants and explaining their roles; and explaining audience roles.

Selecting the Role-Playing Problem

The teacher's first decision involves the selection of the issue or problem to be dealt with in class. Some of the criteria for the problem selection were discussed in Chapter Three, where it became clear that the teacher must consider her own teaching goals and the needs and limitations of her students. Most of the case studies in Chapters Four and Eight are examples of how teachers can start from obvious student problems. Two of the examples in Chapter Eight, those of Mr. Day and Mr. Evans, will illustrate the selection of a role-play strategy on the basis of the teacher's own instructional goals.

An important obligation of the teacher in selecting situations is to ensure the personal security and privacy of each individual involved, especially when reenacting real-life problems. The focus should be on issues of a general nature involving role behavior, not on individual and personal failings or deficiencies. In general, the teacher strives to confront the group with a balance of relevant issues, selecting neither meaningless topics nor situations that are too threatening.

31

The problem situations selected for role playing may vary considerably in their appropriateness according to the developmental stages and cultural backgrounds of the students. Early elementary school children may play other characters with alacrity but have difficulty in differentiating or dissociating themselves from the roles they are playing. Older elementary school and some junior high school students, entering a stage of life where they are quite self-conscious about their body images and sex roles, may experience considerable difficulty in expressing themselves physically in front of others. Further, they may find it very difficult to portray roles of the opposite sex or interact in situations involving members of the opposite sex. Sometimes these youngsters will engage in insightful and relevant monologues but stand stiffly without moving. This may be especially the case with students from middle-class or upper-middle-class homes and backgrounds. Substantial scientific research suggests that children from such familial and community environs may be physically constrained and prefer verbal modes of expression. Lower-class youngsters, on the other hand, often feel more at home with physical modes of expression and self-assertion. When the idea of role playing is clear, these youngsters may be quite comfortable acting out concrete and immediate events and relations. In fact, they may find this technique more suitable for their own styles than the usual classroom emphasis on words and verbal symbols as the learning medium. In view of obvious cultural and developmental differences among children, the teacher must consider these influences carefully in determining the problem situation, the actors or participants, and the particular role-playing format he will use. In some cases he will want to choose situations that are maximally comfortable for himself and his students; in other cases he may prefer to explore difficult situations just because they hold a great potential for learning and growth.

Warm-up

This second step is particularly important in classrooms where role playing is being tried for the first time and with younger children. Sometimes these students may be inhibited in performing in front of their peers or uncomfortable in watching their peers "act." The purpose of a warm-up is to relax all the students and to give them practice and security in public performance and expression. For instance, the teacher might ask the students to smile, chew, or laugh. He might start with a game of charades, which gives both actor and audience practice in communicative skills. In some cases the teacher may actually use props as aids in setting the stage for improvisations. In warming up the class, the teacher should begin simply and may gradually proceed to those exercises requiring greater physical activity or imagination. The Appendix contains numerous examples of warming-up exercises.

Explaining the General Situation

Once the problem has been selected and after the students are sufficiently relaxed and quiet, the teacher should explain the general problem situation to the entire class. The students should understand the educational purposes of the drama and how the issue or problem is relevant to them. Further, it is important for the entire class to know the site, general characterizations, and broad courses of action within the problem situation. This explanation enables all students—actors, observers, and bystanders—to share a common reference and begin from the same understanding of the situation. It also helps involve all the students and lessens problems of wandering attention and boredom.

The explanation to the audience can be relatively brief. (A subsequent section describes the more extensive directions required to brief the audience on specific observational or data-gathering activities.) For example, in introducing a play involving "pencil snitching" the teacher may say:

> Three people are writing themes. Bob is very interested in his theme. Ada feels lively and just for fun takes Bob's pencil. Claude likes Bob and tries to help him get it back.

Or a more complex situation:

> Three students are modeling with clay in a sixth-grade art class. They're making ceramic figures for gifts. The best figure will win a prize. Don is good at art and is making a very good dog. He accepts suggestions but thinks for himself and won't do what another person suggests unless it seems like a good idea. Evelyn is a friend of Don's and will defend him if someone criticizes him. Florence thinks she knows how to help Don, and she goes over and tells him how to do it better.

In certain special circumstances the teacher may prefer to omit this step. He may brief the actors privately and ask the rest of the class to guess at the major issues, roles, and applications. This provocative modification should be attempted, however, only after the class has had some experience in role playing and is able to grasp situations with little orientation.

33

Explaining Participant Roles

To create realistic situations and realistic players, the teacher must be careful to select the proper students to play given roles. It may be a good idea for casting to start with socially competent and respected peer leaders, then move toward the involvement of children in greater need of help. In this way the teacher gains student acceptance of role playing, and both teacher and class can experiment with the more skillful students first. Attention to such problems may avoid the awkwardness of asking for volunteers and having no one speak up because of embarrassment or resistance. If initial requests are made of students who enjoy acting or who have confidence, others will see what is involved and may become more at ease and willing to try a role. The teacher may ask the class to help in selecting participants, just as they helped in problem identification.

The assignment of students to specific roles should avoid placing any child in his usual life role. If the teacher or class assigns a student to a role, the student may feel that he is really like that role and become deeply and personally overinvolved. The actor may think the teacher feels he needs to play the role and may thus feel overly self-conscious about his behavior and easily hurt by class reactions. Such casting generally not only encourages the actor and audience to see that child as his usual self but also focuses attention on the individual rather than on the role he is portraying. If for special reasons a child is cast in a role similar to his real-life role, the teacher should be sensitive to these hazards.

In all circumstances a child should feel free to decline a role if he feels uncomfortable in it. Even if a role-playing session has been specifically designed to help a particular child, it may be better to involve him as an observer or a reactor than as an active participant. Similarly, if the teacher feels that an event that has occurred recently offers a good opportunity for class observation, it is better to cast those students who were directly involved as observers rather than as actors. As observers they are partially insulated from too direct a confrontation and can see how others might have handled the problem situation. In other words, it is best for the student to draw his own conclusions about the relevance of the action for him; he should not be forced to face personal inadequacies with which he cannot yet cope.

The students' taking turns at roles, being chosen by chance, or even volunteering are other ways of dealing with the problem of actor selection without explicit assignment. Sometimes a student who is reluctant to play a role will be just as reluctant to refuse his classmates' request. The teacher must be sensitive to these situations and create an atmosphere in which a student can feel free to say no if he wishes. It may be hard to guarantee such an atmosphere when everyone is excited about the task and wants to cooperate, but neither the teacher nor the group should push members into roles they do not wish to play.

The teacher is now ready to explain in detail exactly what role each participant is to play, a step that is often called "briefing" the actors. Careful attention to detail at this stage will help greatly to minimize student confusion during the acting out and discussion. The better the actor-students understand the parts they are to play, the better they will be able to fit into their roles and the less likely they will be to ignore the roles and respond with their own needs and desires. There is nothing to be lost by children acting out their own needs and desires, for these, too, can be fruitfully used as instructional material. In the process, however, the major lesson the teacher had in mind at the outset might well get sidetracked.

In conjunction with role description should go an identification of the personal feelings and ideas of the characters being portrayed. Such careful delineation makes it easier for the actor to feel his part and to play the role rather than himself. The teacher and the student may find it useful to "build a past," to know or imagine something about the history of the character. This will help the student feel the emotional aspects of his character, rather than understand only the intellectual aspects. In general the more an actor "feels like" his character, the less self-conscious he is likely to be.

A description of the role or of the character's feelings or history may be written out on a slip of paper and given to the actor. The actor may find it helpful to refer to it during the scene. For example, after the general explanation to the class in the illustration involving the art class (page 33), the three students selected to play the roles could be given briefing slips such as these:

DON: You're good at art. You're well along in modeling an Irish setter. You know your own mind and take suggestions if they are good; if not, you do as you please. Evelyn and Florence are also making figures.

EVELYN: You like Don very much. You think the dog he is working on is fine; if someone criticizes him or his work you'll argue with them. Florence is also making a dog.

FLORENCE: You think you know how Don ought to make the dog he is working on. You want to help him to do it better, so you go over to his seat to tell him your ideas.

Such briefing sheets can also provide support for the less confident students. If the teacher then helps the actors get into their roles, he can be more assured that they will faithfully represent the probable behavior of the character they are portraying. Name tags might be used to indicate the name, position, or characteristics of the persons to be portrayed: "Pip," "Fourth-Grader," or "Stubborn." These name tags also help differentiate the actor-student from the role he is playing.

In some instances the teacher can modify this briefing by deliberately giving minimal instructions to the actors. If the problem situation is taken from a literature assignment, minimal instructions can be given, because the roles will be well outlined in the assigned reading (see the case study of Role Playing for English Literature in Chapter Eight). Some teachers may adopt this technique to permit the student greater freedom of expression than he would have if he were tightly confined by the character description. When such minimal instructions are given and completed, other students might then be asked to role-play the same instructions in another way. The resultant differences in individual perceptions and role behaviors based on a single set of instructions can be most useful for stimulating classroom discussion.

A final formality for the teacher is to define the physical area to be used for the improvisation and to specify the props—chairs, books, baseball bats, or whatever—that the actors may use. Often students will enjoy pantomiming certain props rather than using the real objects.

Explaining Audience Roles

As the final step in the preparation and instruction stage, the roles of the audience need to be delineated. The essential problem here is to involve the audience in some educationally fruitful and active manner. This can be done (1) by giving members of the audience specific points to look for, (2) by suggesting that each of them identify with or try to experience the feelings of one or another of the actors, or (3) by assigning some other task that makes each of them responsible for observing some aspect of the action and reporting on it during the subsequent discussion of the drama.

The students who are not acting out dramatic roles can in some cases observe the general interaction of actors, or they can be charged to watch for specific things. In other circumstances the teachers can ask them to be identifiers—to identify with the feelings, thoughts, and actions of one or another of the major role participants. Identifiers differ from observers in the degree of their empathy and sympathy with the action. Such emotional ties may obscure objective observation, but they should highlight other nuances and aspects of the feelings associated with the performance. The identifiers are in a position to lend their interpretations of the feelings and thoughts of each of the actors to the actor's own insights.

36

A challenging modification involves the formation of several committees, or subgroups, with each subgroup observing or identifying with a particular role. In this way small groups of pupils can discuss each actor's motivations and behaviors. Another audience role, that of critic, trains pupils to judge both the dramatic portrayal and the players' handling of the problem itself. Members of the audience can be told they will be asked to replay the problem situation, with previous observers now the actors, and vice versa. The following chapter describes other ways in which nonactors can be highly involved in the action.

Whatever role the teacher decides to assign to the audience, it must be as clearly spelled out in advance as are the actors' roles. A participative role of any sort helps the audience maintain attention and interest in the role-playing session. It also helps bring additional insights and resources to bear upon the discussion and analysis of the role-playing experience.

When the class has been prepared and instructed in the problem to be enacted and the role, as actor or audience, that each student will have, it is ready for the second major stage: the acting out and discussion of the situation.

CHAPTER SIX

The Technique of Role Playing: Dramatic Action and Discussion

As a discretionary step before beginning the improvisation, the actors may find it helpful to rehearse their roles briefly. Rehearsals should not duplicate the role-play scene, but each actor might pretend to be his character at another point in time or space. The teacher might ask the student to do some things "the way this character would do them," perhaps drawing upon the warm-up exercises in the Appendix.

The Role Playing

Although the students should now be well prepared to play their roles, sometimes no amount of briefing or rehearsal enables a team of actors to "carry off" the drama. In some cases the action starts out quickly, as in Mrs. Breen's class; but as Mrs. Adams reported, the action may develop slowly. Sometimes the teacher may even have to intervene at the beginning to get the play started. Such questions as "How does your person feel?" or "How are you going to act now?" may be enough to help an actor pick up the flow of action.

Once the action has started, the students should be given enough time to become thoroughly immersed in the problem situation, and to take full advantage of the situation's promise for creating and learning alternative ways of behaving. The role of the teacher at this stage is one that is not easily spelled out. He must gauge time carefully and not let the drama drag on so long as to lose class interest, but he must let it last long enough to present the problem effectively.

As the main action of the episode progresses, the teacher needs to watch for members who fall out of role and give them the help they need in regaining it. If a boy who is cast in the role of a timid newcomer to the group begins to take a good deal of initiative or uses information about classmates that he would not be in a position to know, the teacher may want to raise a question with the actor. It will do no harm to interrupt the action briefly to give this redirection. It is equally important to watch for members who are in danger of being hurt and to prevent them from being overexposed, whether by their own doing or by the actions of another player. Sudden retreat or pulling out of role, inappropriate flushing, crying, or expressions of anger are usually signs that the pressure has already become too great for young students. An alert director will usually avoid putting students in such situations; but failing this, he will be sensitive to the signs of such psychological pressure before it becomes so great as to cause the student to be unduly embarrassed in front of his classmates.

The teacher must choose between several alternatives with regard to the direction as well as the length of the drama. For instance, in the attempt to portray alternative responses to aggressive behavior, loud talking or yelling might develop between actors in front of the classroom. The teacher might decide to stop this argument immediately; or, since pushing, shoving, or fighting are possible responses to aggression, more fruitful learning might follow from the teacher's noninvolvement other than to prevent actual fighting. The other players and the audience could be drawn into a discussion of whether—and why—yelling or a fight might be an appropriate response. Further and perhaps more important, the feelings of the participants might be explored on the spot, without waiting for conclusion in the usual sense. Depending, of course, upon his original problem, his own desires, and the character of his classroom, the teacher may or may not decide to intervene in the actual playing out of the problem situation. The only necessary intervention is to stop the drama after the main points or behaviors have been observed.

In the simplest model of role playing, such as the examples in Chapter Four, actors who have been briefed perform as the persons they are to represent in a situation with which they have been confronted. These actors then verbalize or dramatize what they think would happen. At first it is best to have only a few actors in the episode. Many players, all trying to talk and act at the same time, may confuse the issue and obscure the main object of the session. This confusion occurred in Mrs. Breen's classroom at first, but she was able to use it constructively later. With increased practice, students and teacher will be able to handle more complex situations, and it may then be desirable to involve more of the class at the same time. Multiple role playing by several teams simultaneously can give each class member the opportunity to play a role or to test his own solution to a problem. Individual insights and results can then be shared through a general discussion of each team's experience.

Some students who are not actors may be more directly involved as consultants to the actors. Such consultants may meet with the actors before the role-playing session and suggest how best to carry out the role. At points in the drama the director may temporarily stop the action and allow the actor to seek advice from his consultants before resuming the session. Since a primary purpose of role playing is to see one's own behavior in new perspective, this effect may be heightened by having one student serve as an alter ego. The alter ego identifies with a character but does not feel personally responsible for him. This relationship may be established by having this student tell the actor what to do and how to react. Then the actor and alter ego can not only observe the effects of their mutual suggestions but also actually experiment with new behaviors.

A way of eliciting both overt behavior and underlying motivations or feelings is to give the actor an opportunity to soliloquize. In this technique the actor interrupts the action and talks directly to the class. By reflecting "out loud" on how the character he is playing feels or thinks, the actor makes additional data available to the audience and to other members of the cast. An alternative to the soliloquy is the appointment of a double or shadow, another excellent means to provide material for the exploration of motives, feelings, and concerns. The double, a type of identifier, is involved right along with the actor and enters the conversation when the play is stopped briefly. He expresses his impressions of the character's private thoughts and reactions rather than his observable actions and statements. The double may be the consultant, but his involvement differs: he steps right into the character role, whereas the consultant remains out of the drama as an adviser to the role player.

A different technique is role reversal, where the role player suddenly switches to play an opposite role. Reversal maximizes the effect of "placing oneself in the other person's shoes." It may become fairly easy for a student to act his part without much personal involvement, but being forced suddenly to cope with his own behavior is another matter. To operate within the other person's framework and have to solve the very problems he himself has created may sharpen issues and extend understanding immeasurably.

Under some circumstances it has proved helpful to divorce the dramatized action from any kind of personality involvement. A situation may be so emotional for the participants or so threatening to one or more class members that it would be difficult for any student to put himself into the role without overacting the part or drawing to himself as a person some of the feelings and emotions projected onto the role. A tool for the solution of this problem is the auxiliary chair technique, in which chairs represent the various characters or behaviors to be portrayed and analyzed.[4] The feelings, actions, thoughts, or words that might ordinarily be assigned to a person are assigned to a chair. Name tags can be attached to the various chairs to differentiate one role from another: A chair's label might be "Snu" (for snooty) or "Agg" (for aggressive); "Doe" might stand for a docile, shy child, "Pass" for the indecisive, unopinionated child. Responses characteristic of these behaviors can be verbally expressed by the teacher while he stands behind the chair in question. The students can then behave toward these chairs as if the chairs were actually exhibiting the behaviors.

The teacher can introduce many of these techniques to enliven and enhance the role-playing episode, though he will want to make sure that the class and the individuals are ready for these specialized assignments. Poorly played roles, long, uninteresting scenes, and fuzzy, unclear, or hazy episodes produce more problems than insights. Scenes are usually ended as soon as the main goals of the episode are achieved, and may need cutting and reestablishing to prevent dragging. Many episodes teach the lesson themselves, and extended action may be only anticlimactic.

Eventually the director will end the role-playing drama and bring the actors back into the class group. It has been suggested earlier that special attention may be needed to help the actor "get out of the role," especially if his role has been a striking one. The teacher may say, "You played that role well, John. Yesterday, you managed a role that was quite different," or "Very good, Mary. Now show us that pretty smile of yours so we won't remember you as a grouch!" Another approach is to discuss other ways in which the same role might be played and have a series of actors each try his hand at a different interpretation. The variety of interpretations may serve to take the focus off the role as it was played by any one student.

These are a few of the many techniques of role playing that can become parts of a teacher's repertoire. Any one technique must be selected for its potential effectiveness as a teaching device in the light of the particular situation and individuals involved. With practice it is likely that any group, regardless of age, will mature in its understanding of, and skill with, the role-playing technique. As a result, students will be able to use it with problems of increasing complexity and with a decreasing need for direction.

Discussion

At the conclusion of the dramatic action the teacher will want to engage the class in discussion. He will help class members review the actions, gather and organize the data that the observers have collected, analyze cause-and-effect relations, and speculate on alternative behavioral patterns. Some of the most crucial learning will occur during this stage of the role-playing process, and the teacher should be prepared to take full advantage of the learning potential of this post-role-playing session. New behaviors can be discussed here, with their advantages and disadvantages given full attention. Creative insights and systematic observations can be brought together and publicly shared. The discussion can help to bring an actor out of his role and back to his "real self" and enables critics and other observers to concentrate on the role behavior and not on the actions or person of the actors.

The post-role-playing discussion can take several forms and involve several different students or groups of students. The role players, the audience, or both can contribute to a critical analysis of the dramatic session. The participants can be asked to soliloquize about their feelings as role players, as pupils experiencing the mind of an "other." Actors can remain in character for a time, or they can drop their roles immediately and become themselves. In some circumstances they can alternate between character and real person. The actors can reintegrate themselves completely into the class and participate in the discussion as ordinary class members, or become a panel of actors serving as resources for class discussion. If the students in the audience were organized in groups as observers or identifiers for the drama, these groups can report to the class, or representatives of each group can form a panel to reflect upon the drama and lessons to be learned from it.

Discussion procedures should always include audience participation. The audience may contribute insightful and analytical comments about either the actors' work or the content of the problem itself. Some of the preliminary issues the actors or the audience might speculate about are (1) how the individual characters were feeling, (2) what the characters wanted in the situation, and (3) why the characters responded in the way they did. If these issues can be understood, subsequent discussion might focus on alternative ways of responding to such interpersonal situations. In most cases the teacher should follow the lead of the discussion and not rub in any learning. Belaboring of the insight by the teacher may make it difficult to accept. The students will learn best when they come to their own or peer-aided learnings.

Another important issue in the discussion process is the need to minimize negative judgment. Students are most likely to share their feelings and ideas sincerely when they know their responses will be accepted without destructive criticism. The most effective work on interpersonal relations and learning can be accomplished in this supportive atmosphere. In some cases it may be better for the discussion to focus on positive suggestions rather than on negative criticism. Young children in particular often model their own behavior on what they see in a role-playing scene. It may be more important for them, therefore, to be exposed in discussion to the positive ways of solving problems and behaving rather than the negative or less desirable behavior in the improvisation. Finally, encouragement and appreciation should constantly be given to all players, for encouragement is needed in learning any new skill.

Class discussion of an episode should not severely criticize or ridicule any one student for the way he played a role or for the suggestions he made, no matter how inadequate or inappropriate either may seem. It is usually better to accept any attempt and then to seek alternative ideas and behaviors for evaluation—or to pass on to something else. Similarly, neither teacher nor class should impose unequivocally right or wrong ways of behaving, but should attempt to introduce the feeling that there are different ways of playing a role, different ways of responding to any situation, and that different results might follow.

A final important focus of this learning experience should be the student's ability to apply the examples and lessons of role behavior to his own interpersonal experiences. The teacher should be prepared to guide the discussion so that essential issues are related to other experiences, particularly those most immediate to the student's life. Without this vital step, even the role-playing experiences may become abstract and meaningless. This process of learning involves two kinds of generalizations: (1) from the play to the student's actual experience and (2) from one experience to analogous experiences. Generalization from play to real life is best fostered in a group discussion that encourages and supports full participation by all students. The class might discuss, for instance, the extent to which the principles observed in playing intergroup conflict are applicable to sports competition or to the treatment of newcomers in the class. This process should clarify private misconceptions so that the educational purposes of the role-playing sessions can be realized. The teacher may openly explore the problem of generalization of learning so that students can be made aware of the next steps they must take to fully capitalize upon their role-playing experiences.

Reenactment

After the discussion, and either before or after the evaluation process discussed in the next chapter, the teacher may decide to take advantage of new insights and alternative suggestions for role behavior by asking students to replay the problem situation. For instance, after yelling or shoving has been played as the response to aggression, the discussion might bring out alternative ways of meeting aggressive behavior. The

43

teacher could take advantage of such suggestions by replaying the situation immediately, with the characters attempting to act upon these new suggestions. This procedure may involve role reversals, where the protagonists shift roles, enabling one participant to learn the feelings of the other. Reenactments may also involve the audience and actor shifting responsibilities. The importance of reenactment is that it gives students an immediate opportunity to experiment with new and alternative behaviors. Thus it takes full advantage of the processes of role playing and group discussion of interpersonal relations for promoting behavioral change. Reenactment is the final step of this process, but it may also inaugurate a new round of discussions and evaluations. The reenactment and evaluation phases can be reversed in certain situations, and in some cases evaluations can be delayed until the class has played several reenactments.

CHAPTER SEVEN

The Technique of Role Playing: Evaluation

No instructional sequence and no plan for action is complete without some attempt to evaluate its effects. Many teachers do reflect upon the efficacy of their educational efforts, but it is important for the teacher to develop some objective measures for evaluating the success or failure of new teaching techniques rather than rely on his own observation and intuition alone. To neglect this important step is to risk seeing progress where there is none or growing discouraged in the face of actual student growth. Such an evaluative process may also help the students to focus upon their learnings from this new experience.*

- How can the teacher tell whether or not the time and energy spent in role playing was worthwhile?
- How can the student know whether or not his participation has been productive?
- How can students and teachers improve their skill as role-playing participants?

These and other questions require careful feedback and evaluation after role-playing sessions.

---

*For a discussion of this evaluative process in teaching, see Schmuck, Chesler, and Lippitt, *Problem Solving to Improve Classroom Learning* (Chicago: Science Research Associates, 1966), another booklet in this series of teacher-resource publications. For an extensive series of diagnostic instruments to evaluate the many objectives of role playing, as well as to identify areas of interpersonal life that may be helped through role playing, see Fox, Luszki, and Schmuck, *Diagnosing Classroom Learning Environments* (Chicago: Science Research Associates, 1966).

Evaluation attempts can serve several more specific purposes, among which might be to provide (1) feedback from students to teacher on how they felt about the session in general and the teacher's role in particular; (2) clues that would lead to improvement in use of the role-playing technique itself; (3) suggestions for new problems or new situations to be role-played; (4) information regarding specific "learnings" or outcomes for the session; (5) guides for the application of learnings from role playing to the classroom situation; and (6) evidence of longer-term changes in student behavior that may grow out of a series of role-playing sessions.

Evaluative Procedures

The teacher can gain an objective evaluation of a session through either discussion or a postsession reaction form. The required information may be derived from simple questions such as "How did you like today's session?" or "How do you like role playing?" Questions can attempt to ascertain the extent to which the objectives of the role-playing session were achieved. Students can be asked to evaluate the experience of role playing itself, the ways actors handled specific interpersonal problems, or the meaning of the experience for their own behavior and intellectual or emotional growth.

A more detailed description of some evaluative procedures may be helpful. A simple way to gather feedback about how pupils felt is the use of a postmeeting reaction form, or PMR. A PMR for very young children might consist of several faces, as shown below. The children are asked to check the face that best shows how they felt about the session as a whole and, with additional rows of faces, about specific aspects of the session.

Another form might ask older students to check their reactions to the role-playing session in such categories as the following:

___I liked it very much.
___I liked it fairly well.

___I'm not sure whether I liked it or not.

___I didn't like it at all.

The teacher may wish to get such responses anonymously to assure honesty, but if he is able to let the students know that their signed replies will be treated fairly and objectively he will be able to supplement his own observations as to which students may need additional support to enter into the role-playing activity.

A teacher can evaluate student reactions by taking systematic notes of the session. One teacher devised the following simple categories to describe the overall interest level and checked the appropriate one after each session.

___Most of them were actively interested in participating.

___Most of them were attentive, watching and listening.

___Most of them were fairly inattentive.

___Most of them actively resisted participation and tended to be disruptive.

She also asked herself for more specific types of information each time:

1. Describe in a sentence or two the student behaviors that best represent the category checked above.
2. Which students did not respond in the same way as the majority of the class? How did these students behave?

By approaching her evaluation with this standardized format, she was able to trace the differing and cumulative effects of role playing on student interest and behavior throughout the year.

Another teacher maintained a standard running measure of his students' role-playing ability. He used the simple categories "very poor," "poor," "average," "good" and "very good." After his junior high school students had become fairly sophisticated in role playing as actors and audience, he duplicated forms on which each of them could rate his peers during a session. He included on this form the following information to help them in forming their judgments:

Category	*Criteria*
Very poor:	Was out of role more than in; played the role very inadequately; did not seem to feel the role.
Poor:	Was out of role quite a bit; played the role in a shallow, unfeeling way; was mostly unspontaneous.

47

Average: Was in role most of the time that he was supposed to be; showed some feeling for the role; was not especially creative or spontaneous in bringing out different facets of the role.

Good: Showed some spontaneity; was creative at times; held the role well; was in role most of the time; was able to play more than one role well.

Very good: Showed real talent and skill in portraying various roles; easily entered the role and created behavior; demonstrated feelings suitable for the role beyond what was described in the briefing.

This teacher was thus able to make periodic checks on the students' skill development from his own reactions and from the data he had collected from student observers. He was also able to check his own observations with the perceptions of his entire class.

Evaluation should also aim toward improving the use of the role-playing technique itself. Informal questions at the end of the session—"How did we do?" or "How could we do it better another time?"—would focus not on the behaviors produced but on the mechanics of conducting the session. The teacher might learn, for example, where and in what ways his design of the problem situation had failed to promote his teaching objectives. Furthermore, he might learn where his instructions had been too vague or too rigid to allow actors and audience the most fruitful carrying out of his intended assignments. Attention might also be given to how well actors stayed within their roles, how perceptive the observers were in seeing what was happening, how smoothly the action proceeded, and how much the actors felt they better understood another person's feelings by playing his role. In this same context students could suggest, verbally or in writing, ideas for new or modified role-playing situations and characterizations.

The overall success of role-playing sessions can be measured by the degree to which the original goals or objectives were reached. If the goals of the session and the plan of evaluation were decided on in advance, a check on actual changes in behavior can be an effective evaluative procedure. Behavioral changes can also be evaluated by keeping brief records of significant incidents in the classroom. For example, if the objective of the role playing was to influence students to become more sensitive to the feelings of a physically disabled student in the room, a good measure of its success would be a record of incidents of interaction between this student and the other students. The observation and recording job would be more manageable if the teacher's change efforts were primarily directed at three or four students. Some teachers may wish to share these observations with their students, and thus lead them to further conscious reflections and efforts to change. Since it is difficult to teach and record class behavior at the same time, teaching colleagues can be asked to sit in and observe classroom activity. These colleagues can then contribute their own, more objective evaluations of classroom activity and progress.

Sometimes progress toward an objective requires measurement over a considerable period of time. If role-playing efforts are directed toward making children more accepting of a shy child, results might be measurable only after several weeks or months. If the teacher discerns a highly structured or centralized pattern of classroom interaction, with an elite or clique of chosen students and a number of rejected students, he might select a more complex objective. Role-playing exercises might focus on creating a more diffuse pattern of social interaction with a wider distribution of friendships and attributed leadership. Progress toward either of these objectives can be measured by repeated administrations of sociometric instruments. The case study of Mrs. Adams' classroom presents an example of this approach to evaluation.

Getting objective evidence about the usefulness of the role-playing session is very important for achieving both teacher and student satisfaction. It serves as a foundation for the continuous adaptation and revision of the technique by the teacher and helps him perfect his skill as a director. Most important, securing evidence about actual changes in students' behavior is an essential link in the total teaching-learning cycle and can provide the direction for future teaching efforts.

Continuing Action

It has already been suggested that the ability to generalize from insights gained in role-playing exercises to other areas of life is a powerful learning medium. A variety of evaluative procedures dealing with this problem are described in the case studies of Mrs. Cox's and Mr. Farley's classrooms in Chapter Eight. One crucial generalization link, outlined in Chapter Two, is the relation between role-playing ability and skills in social interaction. The finest actors are not necessarily the most socially competent students or vice versa, but the ability to understand, feel, and play the role of the other is an index of social maturity and skill. This social skill development is an important aspect of role playing, and it too should be assessed.*

Discussion and evaluation of role playing can lead not only to a consolidation of insights and experiences but also to the planning of new

*For examples of tools to measure social-interaction skills and development, see Fox, Luszki, and Schmuck, op.cit.

learnings, whether by role playing or by other techniques. The class discussion often produces new areas of concern and new problems for consideration. The evaluation, like the original diagnosis, can clarify new class needs and suggest new instructional goals. If original goals have not been reached in one role-playing series, a different type of situation or use of participants might be more successful. If original goals have been reached, the teacher's task becomes to discover new goals and plan strategies to obtain them. Once these new directions have been established, the class can be prepared and instructed and a new teaching-learning cycle begun.

CHAPTER EIGHT

Further Case Studies in Role Playing

Brief examples of the use of role playing to explore a variety of special problems are presented in this chapter. One class is anticipating the admission of several Negro students to a previously all-white school. Two of the examples deal with role playing used to enhance subject-matter learning. The final example illustrates how a teacher has made use of one of the situations listed in the Appendix.

A range of grade levels has been selected for these examples—mid-elementary through high school. All situations except the last are taken from actual classrooms, although some represent a composite of incidents from several classes.

Preparing for Intergroup Situations

In this case the teacher utilized role playing to bring a significant community problem into focus in the classroom. Although this example dealt with Negro-white, or interracial, relations, it could just as easily have involved religious, nationality, or cultural relations problems.

1. *Selecting the role-playing problem.* In accordance with rulings by the school board, several Negro students were soon to enter Mrs. Cox's previously all-white elementary school classroom. She was concerned about the reception these new students would receive both in and out of the classroom, and wanted to reduce any barriers between the old and new students. She decided she would try to set this problem in a more general framework than racial integration, so she began by dealing with problems

51

of new or different students in the classroom.

2. *Warm-up*. Mrs. Cox asked members of the class to suggest ways in which they could help new students feel comfortable in class. She made sure the students named specific events such as class parties. She also emphasized the importance of out-of-classroom activities that might be helpful. Further, Mrs. Cox asked her class to think about what sorts of students or groups of students might be hard for them to accept. Some common stereotypes about rival neighborhood groups and schools were brought out.

After this cognitive exercise Mrs. Cox used role-playing warm-ups. She asked two students to come up in front of the class and pretend to be newcomers. She asked other students to pretend they were old class members and to try to introduce themselves to the newcomers. Then Mrs. Cox asked her students to pair off, with one student in each pair playing the role of an old class member, the other the role of a newcomer. Their task was to introduce themselves and get to know one another. Thus the students began to be aware of the meaning and feeling of playing the role and character of another person.

3. *Explaining the general situation.* The scene was to be the class-room, on the first day new students were to enter. For this example the new students were to be from the same neighborhood as many others in the class; they were students who had a lot in common with the rest of the class.

4. *Explaining participant roles.* Mrs. Cox allowed parts to be chosen without special casting. Several students volunteered to be part of a welcoming committee; others volunteered to try their hand at informally engaging the new students in recess games. It was more difficult to recruit actors for the role of new students, but eventually enough students volunteered.

5. *Explaining audience roles.* Mrs. Cox divided the rest of the class into two groups: one group watched the old students, the other group observed the new students. Each audience group was charged with the responsibilities of (1) observing what each member of their actor team did, (2) evaluating the effect on the comfort of the other students, (3) evaluating the way the actor might have felt while doing this, and (4) suggesting other things that each student could have done to make this introduction period easier.

6. *The role playing.* During the first time around, the action was quite halting and the new students needed a number of cues. Mrs. Cox

finally asked each set of actors to meet with their observers. Together they developed some ideas that, when acted upon, made the relationships in the scene easier and speeded it up.

7. *Discussion.* After the role-playing exercise, the observers and actors gave and received suggestions. Mrs. Cox then explained that all the new students had in this case been from the same background as the rest of the class. What would have happened, what new problems would have arisen, if the new students were not so easily acceptable to the class? In effect, Mrs. Cox took the class back to their earlier discussion of students or groups of students who were different from them or difficult for them to accept.

Mrs. Cox now felt it was time to focus more directly on her original concerns. She asked her class to plan a set of behaviors designed to introduce and accept new students from a different neighborhood. Rather than deal with such differences in the abstract, Mrs. Cox now identified the new group of pupils as Negro.

8. *Reenactment.* The students were able to act out, with some very imaginative ideas, a number of ways of dealing with this new and difficult problem. The observers continued in their now familiar roles.

9. *Evaluation.* Rather than typify or direct her students' responses to the reenactment, Mrs. Cox felt that their spontaneity in giving a diversity of responses would be more fruitful in the actual situation. It could lead to more informal and relaxed ways of dealing with the situation. She felt, however, that the classroom situation lacked two important elements of reality. First, there were no Negroes in the class now; no one could accurately portray the feelings and reactions of the new Negro students. Second, the students had taken little or no account of their parents' reactions to integrated classroom or out-of-classroom activities. Suppose they planned a social gathering, and a parent prevented one of the students from going?

Mrs. Cox decided that such questions, as well as a general evaluation of this lesson, would have to be delayed until the integration of her class began, when she would have some measure of its success. Then, too, she would have to discuss with her students the reactions of people around them and prepare them to meet possible community reactions.

Using Role Playing in the Social Sciences

Role playing can be used in many ways to enrich the subject-matter presentation of academic courses. In this example role playing was used to promote learning in a high school social science class. Certain aspects of the social studies curriculum and parts of the scientific process were highlighted through role playing.

1. *Selecting the role-playing problem.* As part of this social science course, Mr. Day wanted his students to examine community reaction to a current social issue. An issue was at hand in school-community relations —a proposed increase in taxes for the school-district millage. This issue had aroused considerable public controversy and was important for students to learn about.

Mr. Day wanted his students to examine this controversy as scientists might, thus learning about certain scientific procedures as well as the social issues involved. He planned that his students conduct a community survey of people's attitudes about the proposed millage increase. One part of the attitude survey was to be a personal interview with a sampling of the community. Mr. Day was concerned that this interview be accomplished well, so he planned to have his students role-play this crucial step in the survey.

2. *Warm-up.* A warm-up was unnecessary, since the students had had experience with role playing in other classes.

3. *Explaining the general situation.* Mr. Day described the community survey to the class, explaining that the interview was the major data-gathering technique and therefore had to be done well. He then reviewed some of the major problems of the interview situation: ways an interviewer may bias a person's answer; difficulties in introducing and establishing a comfortable rapport; and difficulties in accurate recording of answers. Members of the class were to role-play interview situations in order to bring out problems that might arise during actual interviews.

4. *Explaining participant roles.* Mr. Day split the class into groups of five persons each, with each group working in a different part of the room. In each group were a two-man team of interviewers, an interviewee and his wife, and an observer. The interviewers were to practice a variety of ways of introducing, conducting, and concluding the interview, keeping the above problems in mind. The interviewee and his wife were instructed to respond to the interviewers in ways they felt were appropriate for the scene.

5. *Explaining audience roles.* The members of the class not actively role-playing were the observers of each group. The observers were to watch and comment on the presentation and interaction of the interviewers

and their effect on the interviewees.

6. *The role playing.* In one instance the interviewee and his wife "slammed the door" in the face of overzealous interviewers. Most teams conducted the interviews smoothly after the initial hurdle of introduction.

7. *Discussion.* The class felt they needed help in getting introductions to the persons they were to interview. They suggested the principal supply them with a signed note testifying to their purpose. Some interviewers found that the interviewees wanted to know what was to be done with the results. The class decided they would like to tabulate the data from this survey and report the results to the community. Mr. Day thought that these were sound ideas; he agreed to secure the notes and formed a committee to plan various ways the class might present the results to parents, peers, and the adult community.

8. *Evaluation.* Mr. Day felt that role playing had been exceptionally successful in this instance. Through practice, the students had been able to foresee and perhaps forestall some problems in interviewing. In addition, their role-playing practice gave them some significant insights into the scientific process: they understood the need to systematize and communicate the results of the survey clearly and effectively. As a result, the actual interviewing went smoothly—an adequate testimony to the student's preparation and learning.

Role Playing for English Literature

This case study illustrates further the potential that role playing holds for academic as well as social and interpersonal issues in the classroom. It reports on the use of role playing in a high school English class.

1. *Selecting the role-playing problem.* Mr. Evans was concerned that his students did not seem to pay much attention during certain English lessons. They were uninvolved when reading stories, often did not read the material, and seldom retained the plot or major ideas within the works. He decided to try some role-playing exercises to see whether the literature could be made more real for his students. The class was reading Charles Dickens' *Great Expectations.*

2. *Warm-up.* Mr. Evans selected three of the most popular boys and asked them to come to the front of the room. He instructed them to walk across the room as if they were walking on hard pebbles. Next he asked them to look for a lost puppy at night. Finally he asked them to be three

teammates arguing with a silent umpire over a bad call in a baseball game. Through these activities, which the entire class enjoyed, Mr. Evans and the boys illustrated how simple it was to put oneself into a role-playing situation.

3. *Explaining the general situation.* Since the class was in the middle of *Great Expectations,* Mr. Evans used this book as their starting point to deal with the problems he saw. The first twenty chapters of this novel provide excellent descriptions of the major characters, their roles, and the times. Mr. Evans asked his class not to read beyond Chapter 23. Then he asked for six volunteers to read ahead to Chapter 30. He described for his students the essence of the incident that was to appear in Chapter 25: Pip, now a London gentleman, returned home to visit Joe and Biddy on the occasion of Mrs. Joe's death. How would Pip feel with them now? What would happen between Biddy and Pip?

4. *Explaining participant roles.* Mr. Evans gave minimal instruction at this point, since the major roles were well outlined in the novel. He asked for volunteers to play the three major roles.

5. *Explaining audience roles.* Mr. Evans divided the audience into three parts. The six students who had read ahead formed one group and were to compare the role play with the corresponding scenes in the novel. A second group was to watch for the appropriateness of the interaction as it related to the novel's historical context. The third group was to observe the interaction between Pip, Joe, and Biddy.

6. *The role playing.* In the improvisation Pip greeted Joe affectionately and without pretense. With Biddy, on the other hand, he was quite restrained. He did not mention Mrs. Joe. Joe was quite distressed over his wife's death and spent much time mourning her.

7. *Discussion.* In the discussion Mr. Evans first queried the actors as to their motives and feelings about the direction of the scenes. Then the audience had the opportunity to review alternative behaviors. Finally the group that read ahead presented Dickens' own view of the meeting.

The class spent a long time discussing possible reasons for the differences between the novel and the improvisation. "Things are different now" and "I don't know anybody who behaves like that" were heard often. Mr. Evans gradually brought the discussion around to the general issues of character sympathy and identification in literature. Perhaps Pip, the London gentleman who had left home for great expectations in the city, was a hard character for these students to identify with. "But were you," Mr. Evans asked, "ever ashamed of your parents or grandparents because they seemed to be fuddy-duddies?" This proved to be a very fruitful topic for discussion, since it focused on some issues through which this class could identify with Pip.

8. *Reenactment.* Mr. Evans created other opportunities of this sort with *Great Expectations.* For instance, he asked for people to play Pip, Herbert, and Spider when Pip learns that the convict is a close relative. Then the class read Chapter 28, in which Pip discovers the convict to be his benefactor.

9. *Evaluation.* After several such improvisations, with related readings and discussions, Mr. Evans found his students had become much more involved in the novel. They were far more attentive, and many now wanted to read ahead. They seemed most interested in exploring the reasons for disparities between their own improvisations and the novel's actual events. Moreover, they became conscious of the author's methods of characterization and relating events, of the social and historical contexts of this and other literature, and of the need to actually work at reading and feeling a novel. They did exceptionally well on tests and quizzes.

Teacher Use of the Appendix: Understanding Physical Aggression

This final case, a hypothetical one, is based upon role-playing situation 107 of the Appendix. This example will demonstrate how the Appendix can help in constructing role-playing situations in classrooms. Mr. Farley will be a hypothetical junior high school teacher.

The day before, several of Mr. Farley's students were involved in a fistfight in the schoolyard. According to the teacher on duty, this was not a premeditated fight; it just seemed to break out after a minor squabble on the ball field.

1. *Selecting the role-playing problem.* Mr. Farley decided to try some role playing focused on issues of physical aggression. Rather than repeat the schoolyard incident, he decided to create a new situation that duplicated in some ways the atmosphere and events of the schoolyard. He looked through the Appendix and selected the situation called "Understanding Physical Aggression" as most relevant for his problems.

2. *Warm-up.* Rather than use a dramatic warm-up, Mr. Farley asked his students to take a break and get a drink at the water fountain. In order

to get water, they had to form a line in the hall. Thus the students were actively reminded of what it felt like to stand in line to wait their turns.

3. *Explaining the general situation.* When his students returned from the water fountain, Mr. Farley explained the general situation:

> We've just come back from getting drinks at the water fountain. Many times things happen when we're waiting in that line. People get mad at one another, push one another, and sometimes even fight. This happens not only at the water fountain, but in the schoolyard, on the playground, and even sometimes at home. What we're going to do now is demonstrate one event that can occur when you're in line at the water fountain. Let's all see what we can learn from it. Remember, these things can happen at other places, too.

4. *Explaining participant roles.* Mr. Farley then asked three students to play parts in a drama about people and the water fountain. The volunteers were assigned the fictitious names of Andy, Bruce, and Calvin. Each of the boys got a 5x8 card to wear with his "new" name on it. Mr. Farley asked the three boys to come out into the hall one by one, where he briefed them as follows:

> ANDY: You're thirsty and are just walking over to the fountain for a drink. You're in a bad mood today because you woke up with a headache this morning. You know Bruce, who shows off a lot. Calvin is a good friend. If someone bumps into you, you'll look around and not be happy about it if you think the person did it on purpose. Whatever else you do is up to you.

> BRUCE: You like to horse around, and you're out in the hall when you see Andy walking to the fountain. You like him and want to say hello. You go over and give him a friendly push.

> CALVIN: You're in the hall and see Bruce push Andy in fun. When Andy turns around looking cross you say, "Boy, do you look mad!" You like Bruce.

Mr. Farley slightly modified the instructions given in the Appendix by giving Andy additional latitude in his responses and placing him in a bad mood. This was done to increase the possibility that Andy would really feel angry and that a conflict would develop. These role prescriptions were fairly short and clear, so Mr. Farley did not feel that he needed to write them out.

5. *Explaining audience roles.* Mr. Farley then briefed the audience on their responsibilities.

We're going to observe something happening that I'm sure you've seen happen before, in many different places. This time, let's see what good scientists we can be in observing accurately what is going on. I want to divide the class into three groups. Will this group by the window observe Andy for the next few minutes? I want you to take notes on what you see him say and do and what other people do and say to him. O.K.? In addition, I want you to think about how he is feeling while things are happening. This group by the wall, you will take notes and think about Calvin's reactions. And this group in the middle, you can observe what happens to Bruce. After we're finished, I'll want a report from each group, so take careful notes and pay attention. This is an exercise in seeing how well we can observe and think about problems in common, everyday behavior.

In this manner Mr. Farley involved every student in the dramatic portrayal; moreover, he stressed the importance of learning and practicing the observation of behavior. Mr. Farley should try to capitalize on this experience later in the school year by referring back to this role-playing session to teach important lessons in the scientific study of classroom behavior. Since their own behavior is a fascinating focus of children's fantasy and imagination, it is exciting when examined in objective ways that lead directly to more effective feedback and behavioral change.

With these audience roles firmly fixed, the class was ready for the drama to unfold.

6. *The role playing.* Mr. Farley began the session by designating a chair as the water fountain and asking Andy to start walking toward it. Seconds later Bruce entered and gave Andy a gentle nudge. At this point Mr. Farley cut into the drama and said, "Bruce, you know that's not the way you'd greet Andy if this really were out in the hall. Let's not pretend we're at a tea party. Greet him as Bruce might really do it."

The action was begun again and Bruce entered more energetically into his role, giving Andy a healthy smack on the back. When Andy flared up, Calvin entered the drama, and from there on the actors participated in a lively dialogue that bordered on physical fighting but never quite reached it. Mr. Farley's intervention had encouraged the actors to feel free in expressing themselves in front of the class: after all, the classroom is not really a hallway, nor the chair a water fountain, and they needed extra impetus and energy to overcome that artificiality. Mr. Farley had expected that he would have to encourage freer expression several more times, but the players became involved rather quickly.

Mr. Farley did not cut the action abruptly. Only after the actors had talked themselves out and started to look around the room for cues about how to continue did he call the drama to a close. He then began class discussion of the role-playing session.

7. *Discussion.* Mr. Farley asked each of the three groups of observers to meet by itself, pool the observations of the members, and prepare a brief report of what each character did. He then called the groups together and asked a reporter from each to summarize its discussion. After the three reports had been given, members of the class were permitted to direct questions only to other groups; no questions to the actors were permitted at this point.

When appropriate questions were not asked by the class members, Mr. Farley probed further. How did Andy feel when he turned around and his friend Calvin said "Boy, do you look mad"? How did Bruce feel when he saw how angry Andy was? How did Calvin feel when Andy told him to shut up?

When class members had discussed these and other questions, Mr. Farley permitted questions to be directed to the three actors. Class members were then able to verify how accurately they had observed the characters' behaviors and made assumptions about their feelings.

After the analysis of the situation was completed, Mr. Farley asked the class to consider ways in which occurrences of this sort could be prevented. One student stated that the whole thing could have been prevented if Bruce had kept his hands to himself. Mr. Farley said that this was true, but given Bruce's action, how could the misunderstandings that followed be prevented? Failing prevention, how could the characters explain their feelings and actions to one another? One pupil suggested that Bruce could explain to Andy that he only meant to be friendly and that he knew no other way of expressing himself; then Andy probably would not continue to be upset. Similar steps could have been taken for Calvin's behavior and Andy's reaction.

8. *Evaluation.* Mr. Farley evaluated this role-playing exercise by testing how well his students could generalize to analogous situations. He gave them a sample of the conflict that spurred his original interest in role playing and asked them for suggestions to prevent, explain, or handle the event. After he had received the class's answers, Mr. Farley connected the class drama with the schoolyard fight. He used the students' suggestions as examples of how the lessons they had learned in class might be helpful in situations outside the classroom.

CHAPTER NINE

Summary

This booklet describes role playing, a teaching practice designed to improve the learning atmosphere in the class. All people relate with one another and their environment in systematic and patterned ways. An examination of these patterns of interaction, or roles, constitutes the major task of role playing. The theory of role behavior and role playing was presented with several practical examples and case studies of classroom use.

Role playing can be used in the classroom in many ways. It can be used to increase the efficiency of academic learning through the portrayal of current events or historical circumstances, or through the dramatization of plays or novels. Role playing can also be used to teach about human relations or to diagnose and treat classroom problems in interpersonal and group relations. The drama presents students and teacher with a specimen of human behavior that students can study and use to learn about, and practice, effective interpersonal relations. Teachers can use this specimen to gain information about, and plan change for, the existing social situation in their classroom.

An essential characteristic of the drama is its unstructured nature. The drama is not like a formal play, with full script, structured plot, and planned actions. The unique character of role playing lies in its very reliance upon the participants for action. The actors are presented with the broad outlines of a plot and some role relations. It is up to the actors to place themselves in these character roles and to act out a story spontaneously. The drama is like a real-life experience in the degree to which the actors are involved in their roles. Moreover, each person has a different style and creates his own alternatives in the relatively unstructured role.

A unique advantage of role playing is that it affords students an opportunity to practice new behaviors, thus decreasing the gap between "thinking" and "doing." The raw material for doing comes from the actor's own imagination, the suggestions of his peers in the audience, or the prompting of the teacher-director. Regardless of the source, the student in the drama is being someone else and can safely experiment with new and different ways of meeting pervasive problems and conflicts in social relations. The enriching of academic material with this involving and provocative classroom technique can greatly improve students' interest in, attention to, and learning of curricular work.

It is clear that the teacher, both as curriculum organizer and dramatic director, plays an important role in the eventual success of this learning experience. To be successful, the teacher must be both willing and skillful in his approach to role playing. A three-stage, nine-step procedure for role playing in the classroom was suggested. The teacher initiates this process by preparing and instructing his class. Preparation includes diagnosing classroom needs sufficiently to select a dramatic situation with potential for learning. Students must be introduced to role playing through warm-ups, and must understand both the general situation and the particular roles they may play, either as actors or observers. The second stage, dramatic action and discussion, includes the actual performance and class discussion of the action and its implications for learning. The third stage, evaluation, is an essential component of any teaching-learning experience. Objective evaluation can either precede or follow more refined reenactments of the drama. The crucial process here is one of generalizing from this experience to other feelings and situations from which students can learn and practice new knowledge and new behaviors.

Several means of developing teacher skill for role playing were suggested: reading descriptive materials, gradual introduction into the classroom, eliciting feedback from students, practice with adults, and consultation with colleagues and resource persons. One of the ways to involve other teachers in classroom innovations such as role playing is to ask their advice and aid in preparation. Further, colleagues can be enlisted as classroom observers and may offer helpful suggestions.

In conclusion, the reader is referred to the Appendix and Annotated Bibliography. The bibliography suggests several readings that might be useful to teachers who wish to familiarize themselves with previously published theory, research, and classroom reports. The Appendix lists over one hundred different ideas and situations that may be used in the classroom. Warm-ups, two-man situations, group situations, and problem stories are included in this listing. These situations can be used as they are presented, or they can be modified for use in a particular classroom.

Creative attention to, and modification of, the ideas presented in the Appendix will provide the classroom teacher with a vast body of resources. Careful attention to, and diagnosis of, the classroom situation will provide the teacher with various academic and interpersonal problem situations that can be dramatized and studied to advantage. Step-by-step progress through the various stages of the role-play sequence—from planning through evaluation—should provide the teacher and students with an educative experience in the portrayal, study, and practice of new and effective styles of social behavior.

APPENDIX: RESOURCE MATERIALS FOR ROLE PLAYING

Many types of role-playing exercises are included in this Appendix.* Some are most appropriate for elementary school students, others are designed for intermediate or secondary school students. Many areas of interpersonal, intergroup, community, and academic experience are presented in these examples. They are only examples, however, and the teacher should select those best suited to the needs and abilities of his class, rephrase or modify them, or create new ones as he sees fit.

I. Warm-up Exercises

A. These exercises are basically pantomimic and require a minimum of emotional involvement and expression. They may be effective for freeing inexperienced or withdrawn students to perform in front of their peers. Where multiple endings are given, the teacher can select only those he prefers or give them in succession to one or to different students.

1. Pretend that you are walking: —through very deep snow. —on marbles. —through fallen leaves.
2. Pretend to eat: —an ice-cream cone. —a potato chip. —a lollipop. —a pickle. —a toasted marshmallow. —cotton candy. —a lemon.
3. With another student or in a circle of students, pretend to toss back and forth: —a baseball. —a basketball. —a chunk of ice. —a feather. —a porcupine. —a pillow. —a very hot potato.
4. Show the class what you would do if: —you had just walked five miles. —the temperature got up to 95 in the shade. —you tried to lift some barbells. —you had a blister on your heel but were late for school. —you had a cinder in your eye. —you had to carry a full pail of water without spilling any.
5. Without using any objects, show the class how you: —brush your teeth in the morning. —nail two boards together. —put on a pullover sweater.
6. Stand facing another student. When he makes a movement, pretend that you are his reflection in a mirror. Keep this up until you can do it well, then change roles. Make your moves slowly at first; don't try to trick the other person.
7. Read aloud from one of your schoolbooks, pretending that you have a mouthful: —of marbles. —of straight pins. —of peanut butter.

---

*Some of the exercises were taken from work done by Rosemary Lippitt on NIMH Grant OM 376.

64

B. These exercises require varying degrees of emotional involvement. They can be performed like charades, using movements and facial expressions with few or no words. In some instances the exercises allow the student to express whatever emotion he happens or chooses to show; in other instances the exercise specifies the emotion that is to be shown. The teacher may also begin to develop actor and audience awareness by asking for brief reports on, and observations of, what the actor felt during the exercise.

Show how you feel when:

8. —you get a phone call: someone invites you to a party.
9. —you get a phone call: the dentist tells you that you have an appointment this afternoon.
10. —you are looking out a window and see a little bird hit the glass and fall to the ground.
11. —you look out the window and see it's raining hard (*a*) on the day of the game; (*b*) on the day of your school picnic.
12. —you see a large dog running toward you.
13. —you open a present in a big package.
14. —you find a dead squirrel on the sidewalk.
15. —you find (*a*) a pretty stone; (*b*) a butterfly; (*c*) a bird's nest.
16. —you find your baseball bat is broken.
17. —you find someone has torn several pages out of one of your schoolbooks.
18. —you enter a church or synagogue.
19. —you dance to a fast tune.
20. —you watch a funny movie or read a funny story.
21. —you see people teasing a dog.
22. —you see a friend who has told untrue stories about you.
23. —you get a letter saying you've been accepted by the college of your choice.
24. —you finally get an afterschool job you've wanted for a long time.
25. —you've just failed an important exam.

C. The following situations, which are more complex, will help develop skill in spontaneity and expression of behavior. The teacher can give all the directions at once or part by part as the pantomime progresses. The actor should not stop the action while a direction is being given.

26. You're a young person your own age visiting your grandparents who live near a lake. You've gone fishing and are very happy, thinking of the fun you are having and the fish you are going to catch. You bait your hook, put your line in the water, and wait. You begin to get a little tired of waiting. You get more and more impatient and

disgusted. Suddenly you feel a bite. You hook the fish and reel it in. You have some difficulty landing it. You finally do bring it in successfully. It is a beauty.

27. You're a person about your age who is timid. You're alone in the house comfortably curled up in a chair reading. The rest of the family have gone shopping. It is eight o'clock at night; they aren't expected back till nine, when the shops close. Suddenly you hear a strange noise at the door. You listen, and as you listen you become a little scared. You put down your book and move toward the door, but you're scared to open it. Then the noise stops, and you go back to your reading. You hear the noise again, and this time there is no mistake. Something is there! Finally you muster up courage and open the door cautiously. It is a little stray dog.

28. You're a tightrope walker in a circus. You're a very good tightrope walker and have confidence in your ability, but you know the audience will have more fun watching if you pretend to be anxious and scared. It will create more suspense if you appear about to fall. You're anxious as you approach the ladder, and as you climb up get a little scared. (This is just an act you are putting on for the audience, but you want them to think you are scared, so don't overdo it.) The higher you go, the more scared you seem. You reach the top and anxiously start across the tightrope. You are very cautious. Halfway across you actually do slip and almost fall. You finally make it across and are very relieved.

29. You are a person about your own age, or you can be an older teen-ager. You are dressing for a party. You've just combed your hair, but you don't like the way you look. You are concerned about what will happen when you meet your date.

30. You're a young man or woman about to hang a picture on your wall. You like the picture, decide on a good spot on the wall to hang it, and are very pleased with what you think it will look like. You get a hammer and nail and begin to pound the nail into the wall. You hit your thumb.

31. You're someone your age. One day after school you miss the bus and start walking home. Very tired from walking, you sit down on a park bench. Suddenly you see something in the grass; still tired, but curious, you pick it up. It's a $5 bill.

32. You're a teen-ager walking down a busy city street. In front of you two boys are hitting a smaller boy. As you pass, the smaller boy asks you to help. You ask the bigger boys to stop. They look at you and say, "Go mind your own business." You again ask them to stop.

II. Problem Situations for One Main Character

In the following situations one child can take the primary responsibility for the talking and action; the other person(s) can serve as "props."

A. Situations focused on problems of interpersonal relationships between the child and his peers.

33. Your friend has asked you to go skating. Your mother says you must stay home. You do not want to hurt your friend. Mother is standing near.
34. Some friends have invited you to a show. You have to ask them to wait while you check with your mother to be sure she doesn't expect you to be home this afternoon.
35. You want two friends to work with you on a project. You have to make a map of Alaska.
36. A shy schoolmate has returned after a sickness of several weeks. You want to make him feel at home in school again.
37. You want to help a friend who is unsure of himself and shows off and talks loud.
38 You see one child teasing another.
39. You see two children fighting.
40. A classmate jumps on you or hits you in trying to say hello.
41. You and two friends are holding a club meeting. One of them doesn't say anything.
42. You and a classmate are walking through a department store. He tries to get you to steal something.
43. You're having fun with a friend, but he's too noisy and rough.
44. You're walking home from school and see a boy who is a bully. He hits children or snatches their books.
45. You've never played with a particular classmate, but you'd like him to be your friend.
46. Another student has just torn up the homework you spent all last evening doing.
47. A classmate is trying to boss you around too much.
48. A child grabs the ball during a game and starts to run away.
49. A classmate tries to look at your paper during a test.
50. You've finished your work way ahead of the rest of the class.
51. You meet a friend after you've heard that he has said unpleasant things about you.
52. You approach a classmate who doesn't talk much. You want to find out about his interests and what he likes to do.
53. A classmate of another religion has just had a religious holiday. You want to learn about the event.

54. You want to welcome a new student from a foreign country.

55. Two girls are talking together at a dance. You want to ask one of them to dance with you.

56. A friend takes you aside and tells you a secret so that another friend you're with can't hear.

57. You want to make a shy classmate feel better after she's made a mistake and feels ashamed.

58. You see a teacher with her arms full of books. She needs the door opened. You open the door and ask if you can help her. At that moment a child calls out, "Teacher's pet!"

59. As you come into school a strange student calls out, "I don't like you."

60. A classmate says, "Can't you do better than that?" while you are both drawing pictures. You know that he is really unhappy, and you want to help him.

61. A classmate teases you because you are wearing hand-me-downs.

62. You have won three prizes at a party. Another child hasn't won any. You're just about to win a ring toss when you stop and let him win. What happens then?

63. Two friends ask you to go with them. You want to go but can't, but you want them to know you'd like to go another time.

64. You want to introduce one of your friends to your teacher.

65. You borrowed a pen or pencil from a friend but broke it as you used it. You want to return it and explain that you didn't mean to break it.

66. A classmate tells your best friend that he's too skinny and has legs like matchsticks.

67. You want to get to know a girl in your class.

68. You are arguing with a boy who wants to drop out of high school. You want to persuade him to stay in. Then switch roles.

69. Your friends tease you whenever you volunteer in class. What do you do or say?

B. Situations focused on problems of relations between young people and adults.

70. You want to introduce your parents to your teacher.

71. You have just had a meal at a friend's house and want to thank his parents.

72. Act out how the doctor feels about children, then how your classmates feel about the doctor.

73. Act out how policemen feel about teen-agers, then how your friends feel about policemen.

74. The teacher has accused (*a*) you of doing something that another student did; (*b*) another student of doing something that you did.

75. The teacher has praised (*a*) you for doing something that another

student did; (b) another student for something that you did.

76. The teacher has just made a mistake and you want to point it out to him.

77. You come into class late; it isn't your fault.

78. You have a lesson that you don't understand.

79. Your teacher is very busy and seems to have a headache. You know he doesn't want to talk to you at this moment, but you have something urgent and must approach him.

80. You meet the assistant principal, whom you dislike.

81. Your employer wants you to work overtime the night of a big party.

82. Your father tells you his company is transferring him and the entire family must move to a new city.

83. Your mother wants you to go to a summer camp, but you want to stay home this summer.

84. You are being interviewed for a part-time job (a) as clerk in a store; (b) as a gas station attendant; (c) as a summer camp counselor.

85. You are being interviewed by a professor for admission to the college of your choice.

III. Situations with Alternative Solutions for Two or More Persons

The alternative solutions might be used one at a time, introduced as instructions during the briefing. Evidence could be gathered on how effectively each one works out. They might be shared with the class, serve merely as background information for the teacher as he develops plans for the session, or be introduced into class discussion only after the participants perform their own creative solutions. The purpose of these series of alternatives is to provide a range of potential responses to each situation. There is no necessarily right or wrong solution to any situation.

86. You're talking to a friend about schoolwork when another friend phones to say that he (or she) is coming over. You know that the two friends don't like each other. What can you do?

    Possible solutions: —"Sorry, I'm busy right now. Can you come over tomorrow?" —Ask the friend who is there if he minds the other one coming over (if the other friend is persistent about coming today). —"I wish you could come over but I've got to finish up what I'm doing now." —"Sorry, but so-and-so is here now and I know you don't like him very much. Can you come over tomorrow (or some other definite date)? I'd really like to get together."

87. You have to return a borrowed object that you broke. How do you do this?

Possible solutions: —Apologize for breaking it and offer to replace it. —Apologize for breaking it and, since you have no money right now, offer to make one like it, to replace it when you have some money, or to give something of your own to replace it. —Mend it before returning it and then apologize and ask if this is satisfactory.

88. What can you do when the classroom is very noisy?

Possible solutions: —Ask the teacher if you can go to the library because you have work to do. —Stop making noise yourself. —Politely ask the noisiest pupils to be quieter. —See what is causing the noise and if it is unnecessary noise ask someone to help you quiet the group. —Ask your friends to help you get the group quieter. —Think how the others feel and whether they would like you to ask them to be quiet.

89. A friend returns a library book charged out to you. His little sister or brother upset some water on the book, and it's ruined. What do you do?

Possible solutions: —Accept it with no reference to what happened if he doesn't say anything about it. —Accept it with a nice joke about what happened. —If he explains, accept it with a remark to indicate you understand it could have happened to anybody. —Accept it, but ask if he'll pay for the damage.

90. You want to draw a shy classmate into your project of working on a map.

Possible solutions: —Suggest to the group that the shy person could help with some part of the project, get their backing, and then invite the shy one in. —Ask the shy one if he would like to help, not telling him what to do but asking what he would like to help with. —Show the shy one that you need his help and ask him to give you a hand at the job.

91. You have a friend who is unsure of himself and shows off and talks loud. How can you help him?

Possible solutions: —Take him aside and tell him that you think he had a good idea, but that you don't think he put it over right. —Be interested in what he is talking about and try to find ways of making him more secure, as by telling him about something good that he did. —Build him up; ask others to try too. —Show that you like him. Show your feelings of friendship for him in front of others. You don't have to be so direct as to say "I like Joe" when he's standing there, but you can back him up in something he does or wants. —Introduce another idea or get his attention before he has a chance to show off. Then make him feel at home and wanted.

70   92. You've just been hit hard by a paper wad that was shot at you by

another member of the class. If you tell the teacher, you may get beaten up after class; if you don't tell, you may be hit by another paper wad. What can you do?

 Possible solutions: —Ask the other person to stop. —Tell the teacher, but don't let anyone know you told. —Shoot a paper wad back at the other person. —What other solutions can you think of?

93. You and two other classmates want the same book. What can you do?

 Possible solutions: —Take turns. —Have one read to two others, taking turns as readers. —Choose lots to see who should have it first; the other two get another book to read until it's their turn for this one. —Get another copy of the book. —Find something else to do. —Read it or look at it together.

94. One of the boys in the class has taken your pocketbook and hidden it. You think you know who it is, but when you ask him about it he says that he didn't take it. How can you get it back?

 Possible solutions: —Ask the other students who took it. —Look for it yourself. —Tell the teacher.

IV. Problem Stories for Several Participants

These incomplete stories describe fairly complex problem situations that will hold the interest of a class and provide the basis for group improvisations. The teacher can read the story to himself and explain it to the class or he can read it aloud to the class. For these examples the teacher and class can create their own alternative solutions.

95. *Mary's Art Class*

 Mary was making a vase as a gift for her mother on Mother's Day. It was one of the best in the class. Mary wanted it to be very nice because this year her mother's birthday fell on Mother's Day. She was painting the vase when she heard a shout. She looked up and saw that Jim had upset his paints on the floor. Several children ran to look, and some helped to wipe up the mess. When Mary returned to her desk the vase was gone! She stared in amazement. Then a streak of paint made her look down. It had fallen on the floor and broken. Someone had knocked it off her desk as the children ran to see the paint on the floor. No one had meant to break the vase; it was an accident.

 Act out what you think Mary and the class can do.

 Possible solutions: (*for Mary*)—She could begin to work on a new vase. —If time was short, she could ask the teacher or a a group of her friends to help her make a new one. —She could take the pieces home to her mother and explain what happened. This way she could show her mother that she didn't forget her birthday and that she would bring another vase home as soon as she completed it. —She could get angry and yell or cry.

(*for the class*) —Help her make another one. —Have one of the students offer her his vase. —Take up a collection so that she could buy her mother a present. —Ask the teacher to help her. —Laugh at her problem.

96. *A Parent Steps into the Room*

It was a busy afternoon and the class had worked well. The teacher had promised the group that she would show them a movie. They had just finished their work and were putting their books away to see the movie when Mrs. Brown, Jerry's mother, came in to talk to the teacher. Jerry was out with a cold. His mother had come to pick up the books and assignments for the last week. The teacher and Mrs. Brown stepped out of the room to talk. As she talked with the teacher, the class got more and more irritable and tired of waiting. They'd worked hard and felt they had earned the movie. The clock ticked slowly on and the students feared that it would be time to go home before the movie was finished. Now, the group knows that Frances and Jim will make trouble. Frances will throw a paper wad at Jim. Everyone will laugh and then Jim will throw a paper wad at Frances.

What can the group do to prevent Frances and Jim from acting up? What can Frances and Jim do when they feel like acting up? What can the group do to get the teacher back in the room?

Possible solutions: (for the class) —The class chairman could take over and begin some class game, such as Hangman or Twenty Questions. —Someone could ask whether he could start the movie. —Their friends could ask Frances and Jim to help them with a drawing or an arithmetic problem. —A friend could tell them that their behavior wouldn't be nice, especially since a parent was there, and that their actions may get the entire class into trouble. —The class chairman could ask the teacher if she could take a minute to start the movie and then talk with Mrs. Brown.

(*for Frances and Jim*) —They could work on a paper or do some arithmetic. —They could get a book to read. —They could read a story or ask another to read it to the class.

97. *Sid and Susan Don't Speak*

Sid and Susan had been working with two other students on a big painting for the wall. It was to be shown at the parent-teacher meeting. Sid, who was usually so friendly, passed Susan in the hall one day without speaking. Susan went over to work on the painting with the other children. She had nearly finished her part, but Sid had not done all of his. One of the children called to Sid, "Come on over and get to work. We've got to finish it today." Sid acted as if he didn't hear. He took his arithmetic book up to the teacher. She helped him with a problem, and he sat down to work at his desk. Now the children don't know that Sid's dad has promised him a new bike if he gets all his arithmetic right for a week. He wants the bike very much. He also feels bad because he is not helping on the picture. He feels shy and doesn't know what to do. But the others feel Sid isn't doing his share. One of the boys calls out, "Sid is a quitter!"

How can the group help Sid? What can Sid say to the group?

Possible solutions: (*for the class*) —They could ask Sid why he wasn't helping even though he'd promised to help finish the picture. —They could ask the teacher to make Sid do what he'd promised.

(*for Sid*) —He could explain to them the jam he was in and ask them what they'd suggest he do. —He could realize that he was being selfish and only thinking of himself. —He could explain the situation to the teacher and ask if she could help him after school. In this way he could finish the picture and get the bike. —He could explain the situation to his father and ask him what to do.

(*for Susan*) —She could ask Sid what was bothering him and offer to help. —She could ask the others if they know what's bothering Sid or why he isn't helping them.

98. *The Birthday Party*

JANE (*running up to Mary in a desperate mood*): Oh, Mary, what can I do? I want to invite you and the other girls to my birthday party, but I don't want Sunny.

MARY: I know how you feel. My mother made me invite her to my party and she just ruined it. She came early, and when she met the others at the door she acted great. She said, "Put your coats there, girls," and "Now the presents go on the table in the living room. You sit there," and on and on like that.

JANE: Oh, Mary, it was awful when she took all the cards to read aloud and told you where to sit and how to pass the presents around in a ring. You'd think no one knew anything except her.

MARY: Gee, Jane, you are in a fix. Can't you get someone to invite her out for the day?

Sunny is a pretty blond girl who tries to help all the time. She knows the girls don't like her, so she tries to make them like her by doing things for them. In trying so hard, she bosses them around all the time. Sunny hopes that she'll be invited to Jane's birthday party. In fact, she sees the girls talking on the playground and runs over to them.

MARY: Oh, oh, here she comes!

JANE: What will I say?

SUNNY: Oh, hello, girls.

How can the girls help Sunny act better at parties? What can Sunny do to change? Remember, she wants to help.

Possible solutions: (for the girls) —They could give Sunny a specific job at the party such as taking the coats or folding the paper from the presents. They could explain that some of her other friends were given a job also, so that each girl would have time to participate in the games rather than direct or organize them. —They could compliment Sunny when she arrives at the party to show her that they accept and approve of her.

(for Sunny) —She could be less bossy. —She could ask what she can do to help or wait until she is asked before helping. —She could think of how others feel and what they want from her to have a good time. —She could offer to help Jane's mother with the refreshments. —She could watch the others to see how they act and what they do to help.

99. *John's Choice*

John's best friend, Mark, was about to move away from the school. The class liked Mark and had decided to give him a surprise party. John was excited and helped the class set the plans for Friday afternoon. On Thursday evening John's father came home with tickets for the next afternoon's circus. He knew how much John liked the circus.

John came running home to tell his parents about the party. He was glad to see his father, but then the circus tickets came out of his father's pocket. Now John felt he had to be at the party to say goodbye to Mark. He also wanted to go to the circus. He wanted both things. What do you think John could do?

Possible solutions: —He could explain the conflict to his father and try to get the circus tickets changed for another time. —He could invite Mark over this evening to say goodbye and then go to the circus tomorrow. —He could give up the tickets and go to the party. —He could ask the teacher and the class to change the party to the morning.

100. *The New Snow*

It was like a fairyland as Susan stepped out into the new snow. The sun was shining, and the snow sparkled like jewels. Susan felt it was beautiful. She just stood and looked. Then she saw her friend coming down the street. Yes, she must not be late for school. She walked along with Carolyn and the snow went scrunch-scrunch under their feet. Carolyn was the first to speak. "Hi, Sue, isn't it fun walking to school in the snow?" Susan was still thinking of the lovely sparkles and could not find ways of expressing her feelings. Carolyn looked at her and asked, "Say, what is the matter with you?" Susan replied, "Well, I was just trying to tell you how happy the beautiful new snow makes me feel, but I didn't know how. How could I do it?"

How could the two girls share their joy and wonderful feelings with others?

101. George Gets a New Bike

It was turning cold as George rode his new bike down the street. He was very proud of it and wanted to show it to all the boys and girls in the school. He felt so happy that he whistled as he rolled along. He saw Vernon first and called out, "Hi, Vernon! See my new bike? Isn't it a beauty! It has a light and a horn. Beep, beep!" He was so happy he wanted Vernon to be happy too. Vernon called back, "Oh, a new bike. So what. We all get them. Boy, do you think you're great!" Vernon really had not had a new bike for a long time and he wanted one badly.

How could George share his happiness with Vernon without making Vernon feel unhappy?

102. Jim Tries to Stir Up Interest in Current Affairs

Jim was very interested in current affairs, and he wanted to get other students to help him on a project. The town was soon to vote on a proposal to increase the amount of money for the schools. Jim felt the schools needed more money and wanted to organize some students to ring doorbells and talk to voters about the proposal. When he approached his friend Nancy, she told him she was not interested in helping. She said she had schoolwork to do and wanted to go out later.

How could Jim and some others who feel the way he does convince Nancy and others who feel as she does? Also, how could Jim and his friends approach the voters to talk about the school issue? What problems might they run up against in talking with adults in this way?

103. A Walk to School

Mary rushed through her breakfast. It was already ten after eight and Sally was sure to be there at the usual eight fifteen. She galloped up the stairs two at a time, put on her coat, grabbed her books, and ran downstairs again. "Don't rush like that, Mary," her mother said. "You'll get indigestion." She shook her head as she watched Mary gulping down the last remains of breakfast. "I'm late," Mary sang out as she rushed to the door. Just as she was opening it, putting on her coat at the same time, she saw Sally walking down the street with another girl right opposite her house. She was just about to call out to Sally when she saw that Sally obviously had no intention of stopping by her house as she usually did each morning. Mary was stunned. She felt so terribly hurt she didn't know what to do.

How did Mary feel? What could she do?

104. *Going Skating*

Sally was a very shy girl and often felt left out of things the other children were doing. Martha had invited her to go skating in the park. Sally ran home to get her skates. She changed into her skating clothes and then looked for her skates. They were not in the usual place. Just then her mother ran in from the garage. "Oh, Sally, I'm so glad you're dressed for skating. I've just been given some tickets for the ice show and we can skate for an hour after the show is over. Hurry and get some mittens and we'll go. I've already put your skates in the car."

Sally stopped and stood still. What about Martha? Sally wanted to skate with Martha and she also wanted to go with her mother.

What could Sally do?

105. *Molly and Jim Don't Know How to Act*

Molly was a good student and liked to do her work well. She was also good at sports. She had pretty brown eyes and curly hair. The children liked Molly very much. Jim was also good at sports, and he liked Molly. He wanted to ask Molly to go to the movie with him. Jim came up to her and pulled her hair. He felt awkward in trying to ask her to go with him. Molly liked Jim, but she felt hurt because she thought he was trying to be mean. She felt he did not like her.

What could Jim do to let Molly know he really liked her? Do boys often tease when trying to say hello? Do girls know that the boy who teases is often saying he wants to be friends? Do boys know that their teasing is usually disliked by the girls?

106. *The Grab Bag Party*

Tony's class had planned a grab bag party at school. Each student was to bring a present that cost about fifty cents. Everybody in the class was looking forward to the party. As the class was dismissed, Tony heard his friends laughing and joking about the funny presents they would bring on Friday.

The minute Tony got home he excitedly told his mother about the party plans. He was especially happy about the coming event because his mother never had a party at his house. When Tony told about the grab bag present he was supposed to bring, his mother said, "Well, you'll have to bring your own self and no more." "But Mother," Tony said, "everybody has to bring something. If I don't, then somebody who brought a gift won't get one back." "That's final, Tony. We can't afford to waste money on silly little extras like that, and you know it. Now let's not talk about it anymore."

Tony had to go to the party without a present. Should he embarrass himself by telling the teacher he doesn't have a present? Should he say nothing and be unfair to another student?

107. *Understanding Physical Aggression*

Andy is thirsty and walks over to the drinking fountain for a drink. Bruce, who enjoys horsing around, sees Andy and wants to say hello. He goes over and gives Andy, whom he likes, a push. Calvin, a good friend of Andy's, sees Bruce push him, and when Andy turns around Calvin says, "Boy, do you look mad!"

What did Bruce do when he saw how Andy felt? What could the three do to replay it so that the ending is not so difficult? What can Calvin do and say when he comes up and finds this kind of situation? How can simple misunderstandings like this be prevented or explained when they do happen?

108. Many frequently studied novels or plays can be selectively role-played, just as Mr. Evans did with *Great Expectations.* Here are some examples:

From *Johnny Tremain:* Act out what Johnny would have been like at the onset of the American Revolution, had he not burned his hand and had he remained with the Laphams as a silversmith.

From *Romeo and Juliet:* Act out what might have happened had Juliet told her parents in Act II that she was going to marry Romeo against their traditions and wishes.

109. The lobbying process is part of the functioning of American political decision making. Create a scene in which a lobbyist wants to push a bill to give special advantages to lumbering interests. He approaches two congressmen, one from Washington or Oregon and the other from Arizona.

V. Situations Dealing Directly with Sensitive Interpersonal or Community Issues

Role playing presents an opportunity for direct confrontation with, and learning about, important issues in an educationally supportive atmosphere. But careful groundwork must be laid before sensitive issues can be dealt with fruitfully. Community support, educational relevance, and a high degree of teacher skill and teacher-student rapport are vital for effective work in controversial areas. Many problems that arise in such sensitive and controversial areas are dealt with only correctively, through counseling or punishment. Through classroom role playing, the problems implicit in parent-child relations, value conflicts, racial relations, and dating and sex relations can be observed and discussed. By bringing feelings out into the open, and by considering and evaluating various alternative behaviors, students will be able to face the realities of their worlds with greater understanding and skill.

When the community, teacher, and students are prepared to deal with sensitive or controversial issues, the following examples may be helpful. Since controversy is subjective, some of these examples may appear uncontroversial to some people and too controversial to others. Each teacher will be required to make his own sensitive judgment for his own case.

110. You want to make a new student feel at ease in the school. He is the only Negro in the class.

111. You want to tell your date that you had a good time and like him (her).

112. You want to tell your boy friend (girl friend) you don't want to go steady anymore.

113. You want to go to church, but your friends are trying to persuade you to play baseball this Sunday morning. They don't understand why you want to go to church.

114. You and some friends want to play baseball and want another friend to join you. He wants to go to church and doesn't understand why you don't want to go.

115. Your parents tell you that they don't approve of some of your friends of the same sex. They think these friends are a bad influence on you and insist that you stop seeing them. You like these friends, enjoy being with them, and want to continue to see them. What can you do to influence your parents? Enact the scene where you and your parents discuss this problem.

116. You tried to help get your friend elected president of a club in school, but your friend lost. The new president is of the Jewish faith, and your friend says, "Now that bunch is going to form a clique, and he's going to appoint all his friends to the important jobs." How can you deal with this situation?

   Possible solutions: —Agree with your friend because he's right. —Agree with your friend because otherwise he might dislike you. —Disagree with your friend; tell him it's a case of sour grapes. —Agree with your friend because it's the simplest thing to do; it's too hard to change the feelings or prejudices of others.

117. You become friendly with a pupil in the class and want to bring him home for dinner. The new classmate is a member of a different race, however, and your mother refuses to let you bring him to your house. What can you do?

   Possible solutions: —Give up your new friend. —Ask your

teacher to talk with your mother. —Ask your mother why she feels this way. —Tell your mother she's prejudiced. —Arrange some way your mother can meet your friend.

118. Your parents insist that you come home from a date earlier than you want to. What can you do?

   Possible solutions: —Obey them without any discussion or argument. —Just stay out at late as you wish. —Introduce them to your date and ask permission to be out later. —Discuss it with them, giving all the reasons you can think of. —Get your friends to help you convince your parents. —Find out why they feel the way they do. —Tell your date you have terrible parents and must come home early.

   What can you do if you have tried some of these solutions and neither your parents nor you have changed your mind?

119. A young boy, about fourteen, is in the courtroom for stealing some groceries from a large store to get food for himself and his family. The main characters are the judge, the boy, the boy's mother, a lawyer defending the boy, and a lawyer prosecuting the case. The scene can be acted out by high school students with minimal instructions and no prearranged dialogue. The discussion can concentrate on the attitudes other students have regarding this situation or on the feelings of each actor as he approaches this event.

120. A young boy, about ten, is caught by the manager as he steals some candy and a water pistol from a small store. The store is in a good neighborhood, one in which the manager knows the parents could afford to buy such items. What does the manager do? How does the boy feel?

121. You are a good student and are working on a very difficult test the teacher has given to the class. Your best friend, Robert, who is sitting next to you, leans over to try and see your answer to one of the questions. What do you do?

   In the same testing situation Robert tries to get help from someone else, and he gets the answer from that person. You see this happen. What do you do?

   (Both these episodes can be replayed with Robert as the class leader, the teacher's pet, or a pupil nobody likes.)

122. Your junior high school has just made a regulation that girls' skirts should cover the knee. You have just bought a very pretty skirt that is shorter than the rules permit; it ends one inch above the knee. Your mother says it's fine with her if you wear it. What happens in the classroom when your teacher notices the length of your skirt?

123. Your junior high school has just made a regulation that boys must keep their hair neatly trimmed. You like your hair long and your

family doesn't care. You feel you have a right to wear your hair any way you wish. What happens in the classroom when your teacher notices the length of your hair?

124. You are sixteen years old, but a little short for your age. You and your parents are going to the neighborhood movie theater, where youngsters fourteen years old and younger are admitted for half price. Your father buys tickets for two adults and a child. When the cashier asks how old you are, your father answers, "Thirteen." What do you do?

125. One of your teachers is well known for her tendency to assign too much work. Everyone, good students and poor students, agree that this is true. Using role playing, test out several alternative ways a small group of students might deal with this situation.

126. We hear a lot about discussions and negotiations to help resolve the problem of some schools being all Negro, or predominantly Negro, just because most of the Negroes live in one section of town. One such negotiation might involve the following characters: a vigorous Negro leader, the mayor of a small city, and the superintendent of schools.

The action can be played first in a Northern city and then in a Southern city. The mayor and school superintendent can be on either one side or the other. Try it several ways.

The action should be reviewed to see how well each character has marshaled facts, arguments, and explanations for his position. Do the actors stay in character during the drama? How does the audience feel about these issues? Could this scene ever take place in this town? The teacher should use this experience to help his class understand current events and the human feelings underlying these current events.

ANNOTATED BIBLIOGRAPHY

Reports on the Classroom Use of Role Playing

1. COOK, M., and TREGAWLYN, J. "Instructions to Teachers from a Unit, 'An Intercultural Action Technique for the Secondary School,'" *Sociatry*, 1948, 2, 281–83. The authors describe a variation of role playing that they used to teach current events. The method was "the living newspaper," in which news situations were acted out in order to make the news more dramatic, impressive, and personally meaningful. They found better attention to, and retention of, news items in their class as a result of the portrayals.
2. KAY, L., and SCHICK, J. "Role Playing as a Teaching Aid," *Sociometry*, 1946, 9, 263–74. The authors describe the use of role playing as an aid in teaching intergroup psychology and child psychology in college.
3. LIPPITT R., LIPPITT, P., and FOX, R. "Children Look at Their Own Behavior," *N.E.A. Journal*, September 1964, 14–16. This article stresses the importance of learning by observing and doing. The laboratory method of social science instruction, including the presentation of samples of behavior through the role-playing exercise, is suggested as appropriate for children in the elementary grades. After the presentation of events or incidents, the classroom teacher leads her pupils through a scientific analysis of the behavior observed. Causal hypotheses about the whys of behavior are discussed and evaluated. The authors conclude: "The children are discovering that there is no subject more exciting to study than the behavior of themselves and others."
4. LIPPITT, ROSEMARY. "The Auxiliary Chair Technique," *Group Psychotherapy*, 1958, 11, 8–23. The author describes a variation on role playing for teaching interpersonal relations in the classroom. An auxiliary chair is placed in the front of the room, and human characteristics are assigned to it; then children behave toward the chair as they would to a person with these characteristics. For instance, the chair could be an aggressive younger brother, and the schoolchild role-plays how he would handle this sibling. The auxiliary-chair technique provides protection of persons by focusing emotions on the chair, thus allowing greater objectivity in dealing with behavior. The author reports great success in her work with younger children and gives many examples and suggestions.
5. LIPPITT, ROSEMARY, and HUBBELL, ANNE. "Role Playing for Personnel and Guidance Workers," *Group Psychotherapy*, 1956, 9, 89-114. The authors present a systematic and comprehensive review of both published and unpublished reports of role playing in the classroom. Lippitt describes some of her own work in elementary classrooms. For instance, poor handwriters had less difficulty after the more apt members of the class role-played their approach and method. Observing other children brought improvement in such skill areas as holding the pencil in a relaxed manner, not worrying about mistakes, and concentrating on the work. Lippitt also used role playing in the teaching of literature; she found that when students experienced the emotional situations depicted in the readings through role playing, the material sprang to life for them. In teaching biology she asked students to visualize sequoia trees, to act out cutting through the trees, and to pretend to examine a stump to determine its age. The article contains many examples that demonstrate the utility of role playing for teaching textbook facts and lessons as well as interpersonal skills. It contains many helpful suggestions about skills and techniques that can be used by teachers in the younger grades.
6. MORENO, J. L. *Psychodrama.* New York: Beacon House, 1946. This book contains especially valuable information about the development of social relationships and the relevance of role playing in many areas. The author is a pioneer in the use of role playing as a psychotherapeutic technique for emo-

tionally disturbed persons. His books, speeches, and role-playing reports have helped popularize the technique for workers in other fields, such as industry and education. In this book he reports some results of role playing tried in the classroom. He states that successful use of the technique gives each child greater insight and understanding of his fellows. When the child observes other children acting out their reactions to such typical school situations as unfairness in games, cheating, or pushing in front of others, he realizes that the problems of others are the same as his own. This realization is a common bond that draws the entire class together and improves their mutual liking and morale. High group morale and cohesiveness are seen as positive influences upon learning.

7. SARBIN, T. "Spontaneity Training of the Feeble-minded" in *Group Psychotherapy,* ed J. MORENO. New York: Beacon House, 1946. The author reports work with retarded children in which he encouraged the students to act out roles they saw in everyday life, such as the behavior of a farmer or a delivery boy. After the drama the other students discussed and criticized the behavior, and then were led to enact other jobs incumbent upon the role of being a farmer. This spontaneous use of the children's own resources worked better than usual instructional devices in helping these children of lower intelligence respond to, and learn about, everyday social events.

8. SHORT, R. "Role Playing in Adult Spanish Classes," *Sociatry,* 1948, 2, 333–35. The author reports her attempts to utilize role playing as an aid in teaching Spanish. She found that it improved her class's performance.

9. SOUERWINE, A. A., and CONWAY, K. L. "The Effects of Role Playing upon the Social Atmosphere of a Small Group of Sixth Grade Children." Unpublished paper read at a meeting of the American Psychological Association, 1953. The authors experimented with the effect of role playing upon the selection of friends in a classroom. They found that role playing improved the social atmosphere of the group and increased peer acceptance for all members: many of those formerly isolated and rejected by the class were chosen as friends in sociometric tests administered after the role-playing experiences. Such devices are discussed as one way the classroom teacher can evaluate the role-playing experience.

Theory and Research from Many Fields

10. BAVELAS, A. "Role Playing and Management Training," *Sociatry,* 1947, 1, 183–91. Working with industrial personnel, the author found that workers tend to make the same mistakes during role playing that they unconsciously make on the job. Immediately after the session is over, however, the worker is often able to point out his own mistakes. The conclusion is that role playing is an effective technique for sensitizing persons to their own behavior.

11. BORGATTA, E. "An Analysis of Three Levels of Response," *Sociometry,* 1951, 14, 267–315. The author describes systematic research on experimental discussion groups. When groups role-played a situation, members tended to be much freer and more relaxed in expressing ideas, convictions, agreement, and disagreement. The difference is attributed to the reduction of some of the usual pressures of reality in the role-playing situation, which allows participants to be more honest with themselves and others.

12. COOLEY, C. H. *Human Nature and the Social Order.* New York: Scribner, 1922. In Chapters V and VI Cooley develops the concept of the "social self." The person's concept of himself as a social being arises in a "looking glass" fashion in three steps: (1) how he imagines he looks to others, (2) his estimate of their reaction to this image, and (3) his emotional reaction to this estimate. Cooley suggests that out of these processes the person develops

a coherent and consistent understanding of himself. This book is an epochal work in sociological thinking about the growth of personality and social interaction.

13. DYMOND, R. A. "Preliminary Investigation of the Relation of Insight and Empathy," *Journal of Consulting Psychology*, 1948, 12, 228–33. The author suggests that conscious awareness of one's relations with another person is closely related to the knowledge of the thoughts and feelings of that person. The ability to play the role of the other, as in role playing, is seen to be related to one's insight into personal and interpersonal relations. In later experiments and reports this author attempted to test these ideas empirically.

14. FRENCH, J. R. P. "Role Playing as a Method of Training Foremen," in *Group Psychotherapy*, ed. J. MORENO. New York: Beacon House, 1946. The author used role playing to train adult Boy Scout leaders in democratic leadership. He found that the technique was especially helpful in sensitizing autocratic leaders to democratic methods. Further, the use of role playing for practicing leader behavior helped in the teaching of new methods of discussion leadership and in changing troop leaders' attitudes toward their roles.

15. GLIDEWELL, J. (ed.). *Journal of Social Issues*, 1959, 15, No. 1. This issue of the journal, devoted to "Mental Health in the Classroom," describes several reports of research and action in classroom mental health. The authors stress an interactional view of the student, noting that the child's view of himself, his attitudes toward schooling, and his role in the classroom student group are all interrelated. The issue is a useful compendium of research ideas and results.

16. LUSZKI, M. B. "Empathic Ability and Social Perception." Unpublished doctoral dissertation, University of Michigan, 1951. The author found a positive relation (association) between one's sensitivity to the feelings of others and one's ability to understand objectively what is happening in a role-playing session. The implications are that sensitivity and objectivity training in role playing can lead to greater empathy in interpersonal relations. Sensitivity to the feelings of others seems to involve two skills relevant to the role-playing experience: (1) the ability to identify with others and put oneself in their place and (2) the ability to see oneself as others see one.

17. MAIER, N. R. F. *Principles of Human Relations: Applications to Management.* New York: Wiley, 1952. The author is primarily interested in the application of role playing to industry and to labor-management relations. He describes a number of case studies in which role playing enabled each party to better understand the other's point of view. Several major conflicts and misunderstandings were resolved through the use of this technique.

18. MANN, J. "Experimental Evaluations of Role Playing," *Psychological Bulletin*, 1956, 53, 227–35. The author reviews articles and reports of psychological experiments that have attempted to evaluate the effect of role playing. He summarizes the uses of role playing as (1) a diagnostic assessment procedure and (2) a method for producing personality or behavorial change. The author suggests that many more objective evaluative reports are needed.

19. MEAD, G. H. *Mind, Self and Society.* Chicago: Univ. of Chicago Press, 1934. This book is a landmark in the history of social and psychological thought. Mead stresses the importance of "learning the role of the other" in social development. For interpersonal communication to occur, a person must be able to anticipate the thought processes and the intentions of others. Children's games are suggested as prototypes for learned role behavior.

20. MILLER, N., and DOLLARD, J. *Social Learning and Imitation.* New Haven: Yale Univ. Press, 1941. The authors present a behavioristic-psychological approach to child development. The child learns to behave as an adult principally through imitation of the behavior of persons around him. This is especially true when he is rewarded or praised for such new behavior. Positive

experience with the imitation of new forms of behavior demonstrated in role playing can be an important impetus to behavioral change.

21. MORENO, FLORENCE. "Psychodrama in the Neighborhood," *Sociatry,* 1947, 1, 168–78. The author reports her successful use of role playing in working with ethnic, social class, and marital problems in the community. Parents and children from different families came together for a large session. First the children played roles, acting out taunting and jesting behavior. When asked why they treated their companions this way, they revealed their feeling that their parents did not want them to play with certain boys and girls. The parents, who thought that they had successfully hidden their prejudices, were surprised to discover that their children were so sensitive. The parents exchanged roles with each other, increasing mutual understanding between families. In this report Moreno shows how role playing can be used as a part of a sequence designed to demonstrate problems and discover solutions in community living.

22. ROSENBERG, P. "Some Notes on How to Use Role Playing." Mimeographed report, National Training Laboratories, Washington, D.C., 1950. The author studied the degree of involvement of actors and audience in role playing. She found that individuals who were more highly involved differed in several ways from those who were less involved. The most adequate group experience seems to include some very highly involved actors and some less involved observers or objective audience members.

23. TROW, C., ZANDER, A., MORSE, W., and JENKINS, D. "Psychology of Group Behavior: The Class as a Group," *Journal of Educational Psychology,* 1950, 41, 322–38. The authors present the basic theory of the class as a specific case of a social group. The teacher is viewed as a member of this group, a member with some special responsibilities: classroom management, instruction, and maintenance of democratic classroom behavior. The authors suggest that role playing is one of several techniques of classroom management and teaching that use the results of research in education and psychology to advantage in the classroom.

Other Resources for the Teacher

24. KLEIN, A. F. *How to Use Role Playing Effectively.* New York: Association Press, 1959. This is a short book adapted from a larger volume, but it effectively stresses the utility of role playing for human relations and leadership training. Although not specifically directed at the problems and practices of the classroom, the book contains many useful suggestions for the director or teacher in leading role-playing sessions and demonstrates the utility of the technique for industrial and community organizations.

25. SHAFTEL, G., and SHAFTEL, FANNY. *Role Playing the Problem Story.* New York: National Conference of Christians and Jews, 1952. This pamphlet suggests the utility of role playing as an approach to dealing with human-relations problems in the classroom. The authors describe in detail each phase of the role-playing sequence, stressing especially problems in intergroup relations.

The two other booklets in this series of TEACHER RESOURCE BOOKLETS ON CLASSROOM SOCIAL RELATIONS AND LEARNING are listed below. They discuss role playing in more general terms—as one of several teaching innovations that may lead to improved social relations and learning. For a more detailed description of these two sources, see the preface of this booklet.

26. FOX, R., LUSZKI, M. B., and SCHMUCK, R. *Diagnosing Classroom Learning Environments.* Chicago: Science Research Associates, 1966.

27. SCHMUCK, R., CHESLER, M., and LIPPITT, R. *Problem Solving to Improve Classroom Learning.* Chicago: Science Research Associates, 1966.

INDEX OF QUESTIONS

This index is essentially a list of questions that teachers often ask about role playing.